WHAT'S YOUR PLEASURE?

Playing dress up. Or playing doctor.

Telling X-rated bedtime stories. Or turning an ordinary bedroom into a boudoir that would make the Happy Hooker blush.

Navigating naughty computer games. Or sampling toys that only come wrapped in plain brown wrappers.

No matter your taste, whatever your fantasy, you'll find it in COME PLAY WITH ME. Try it on. Take a chance. Treat yourself. And the one you love. Your sex life will never be the same . . .

ALSO BY JOAN ELIZABETH LLOYD

Nice Couples Do

and

If It Feels Good

JOAN ELIZABETH LLOYD is a former school teacher who lives outside of New York City. Of herself, she says, "Like 'J,' the author of *The Sensuous Woman*, I'm someone who stumbled on new activities to increase the range of my sexual activity. And I've found a new way to communicate with my sexual partner—a way that works. I wrote this book to share with you the wonderful things I've learned."

Come Play With Me

GAMES AND TOYS FOR
CREATIVE LOVERS

JOAN ELIZABETH LLOYD

WARNER BOOKS

A Time Warner Company

Warner Books, Inc., 1271 Avenue of the Americas, New York, NY 10020
w A Time Warner Company

Printed in the United States of America

ISBN 0-446-39538-2

Book design by Giorgetta Bell McRee
Cover design by Julia Kushnirsky
Cover photography by Barnaby Hall

This book is dedicated to Ed.

Together we've traveled the road
from plain vanilla to heavenly hash
with open minds and loving hearts.
And had lots of fun doing it.

CONTENTS

AUTHOR'S NOTE

The book you are about to read is about erotic toys and sexual game playing. There is a warning I must give you before you begin.

These games are to be played only between two consenting adults.

Consenting adults: Both of those words are important.

Consenting: Both parties must understand before they begin that either has the right to stop the game at any time. As a matter of fact, each has the obligation to stop whenever he or she gets the feeling that things have gotten even a tiny bit uncomfortable. If you cannot stop when asked, or if you're not sure whether you are able to say stop when you want to, *don't play.*

Adults: This book is written for grown-ups, both in terms of years and attitudes. Children shouldn't play. This refers to those underage as well as those who lack the maturity to understand that a game is for mutual enjoyment, not to coerce a partner to do anything that makes him or her uncomfortable. If you're not sure of your own maturity, or if you don't trust your partner's, *don't play.*

If you and your partner are consenting adults, however, read on. Come play with me.

LET'S PLAY HIDE-AND-SEEK

SHE: I'm hiding
HE: I'll find you.
SHE: I'm hiding.
HE: I'll find you.
SHE: I'm hiding.
HE: I'll find you and fuck your brains out!
SHE: I'm hiding in the closet.

INTRODUCTION

PAM AND WARREN'S STORY

Pam looked at the three cards displayed in front of her on the folding table, then lifted the corners of her two hole cards and peeked at them again: two pair, sevens and threes. She looked at Warren's cards. She could see a king and jack of hearts and a four of clubs. "I'll raise you ten." She flipped the last of her chips into the pile in the center of the table.

"You've got a pair of sevens showing. Hmmm. Well, I'm feeling brave. I'll see your ten chips, just to look at one more card."

He picked up the deck and dealt her a card. "A deuce. No help." He placed a card next to his. "Five of spades. No help, either. The bet's to you."

"I'm out of chips," she said.

Warren looked across the table. He and Pam had been

dating for six months and had been lovers for the last few months. They had even begun talking about moving in together in the near future. Their sex life was wonderful, rewarding, and satisfying, but a bit tame. Except for two occasions he could remember in detail, their lovemaking had been plain vanilla, in the bedroom, at night. Dreamily, he remembered the two evenings when, after a bit of persuasion, Pam had abandoned her usual restraint and revealed a hint of the sexual being underneath her somewhat prim exterior.

He looked over her turtleneck sweater and jeans. "Okay, let's see. How about this? If you lose, you can give me your sweater."

"You've got to be kidding. You're talking about strip poker."

"I guess that's what it comes down to."

Pam was deliciously horrified. She came from a very rigid background and had been taught that sex was very serious and private. Recently, however, she had begun to question her long-held beliefs. Warren had been showing her how sex could be a wonderful sharing between two people who love each other the way they did. It could be free and spontaneous and lots of fun. "But it's Saturday afternoon."

"It sure is." He looked down at his watch. "Exactly two-forty-three. What does that have to do with things?"

"And the sun's shining."

Warren looked out their fifty-story window. "It certainly is. Shining brightly. But so what? No one can see in."

Pam looked at her cards again. Well, she thought, I'm wearing a bra. "Okay."

Warren dealt them each one last card, facedown. "Down and dirty," he said with a wink.

Slowly, Pam lifted her last card and looked at it. It was a ten. She flipped her cards. "Two pair."

Warren turned all his cards faceup. "Nice. Unfortunately, I seem to have three twos. Your sweater, please."

"Oh, come on. You can't be serious. Not really." She couldn't decide whether or not she wanted to be daring and remove her sweater.

"Yes, really. You lost, so pay up."

Pam felt her face flush. She knew that she could say no and Warren would be disappointed but not angry. Suddenly, however, it felt terrific to be free. She reached down, slowly pulled her sweater off over her head, and tossed it onto the sofa.

Although he was very excited by the sight of Pam sitting half-dressed across from him, Warren tried not to spook her. "You mustn't be ashamed of your body, you know," he said. "I've seen you wearing a lot less than that. Anyway, I love that bra." Pam looked at her almost-flat chest. The bra that kept her protected from Warren's gaze was nothing more than a tiny wisp of lace and fabric.

"I guess I always thought that this kind of thing was dirty. Nice girls aren't supposed to display themselves for men," she said.

"Nonsense. You have a beautiful body," Warren countered.

"Not really. I'm too skinny and my ribs and shoulder blades stick out."

"To me, you're the most beautiful woman I've seen. So don't argue."

Warren got up and opened the blinds all the way. The

sun spilled over Pam's body and he stared. "You look great. And I can see your nipples clearly." When Pam blushed, he said seriously, "Don't be so prudish. You're lovely in the dark and lovely in the sunshine."

Pam cleared her throat. "All right, all right. When you're through ogling my body," she said, sighing, "give me the cards. Sitting here like this is making me very uncomfortable. I want to get my sweater back and it's my deal." It was making her uncomfortable, but it was also getting her very excited.

She dealt the next hand and lost her shoes.

Warren dealt the next hand. By the time they each had five cards, Pam had three jacks and had wagered her socks and jewelry. "I want to bet again," she said.

"With what?" Warren asked. "You haven't got much left."

Pam looked down and sighed. She was deliciously nervous. "My bra."

"Okay." Warren pushed a pile of chips into the center of the table. Then, before Pam could lose her nerve, Warren dealt their sixth and seventh cards. She looked down and saw that she had been dealt a second six. Wow, she thought. A full house. She turned her cards over with a grin.

"Nice," Warren said as he rearranged his cards on the table. "Unfortunately, I have here the seven, eight, nine, ten, and jack of hearts. Seems I've won again."

Pam stared at Warren's cards. "You must have cheated." She looked at Warren. "Forget I said that. I know you don't cheat."

"Your jewelry, socks, and bra, please."

She pulled off her watch, earrings, and socks, then hesitated. "Come on, Warren. Won't you settle for this?

Please." Sitting without her sweater was one thing, but she didn't think she was ready to be naked.

Warren just held out his hand, waiting for Pam to put the wisp of fabric in it. "Not welshing, are you?"

Pam looked at the soft, loving expression on Warren's face and it was suddenly all right. She shook her head and smiled. "Nope, not welshing at all." Slowly, she reached around and unhooked her bra. With an embarrassed grin, she dropped the straps from her shoulders and removed the garment.

"Oh, darling," Warren whispered. "I never realized how beautiful you would be in the sunlight." He couldn't resist pushing her sensuality just a little. "Close your eyes." When she complied, he asked, "Can you feel the sun's heat on your flesh?" He watched her nipples pucker at his smoothly spoken words. He leaned forward and blew on her chest. "Wonderful. Just wonderful."

"I feel so slutty this way," Pam said, opening her eyes, "sitting here naked with the sun shining on me and you looking at me like that."

"Like what?"

"Like . . . I don't know."

"Yes you do. I'm looking at you like you're a beautiful, enticing woman whom I want to make love to right here and right now." Without giving her time to think, Warren stood up and quickly stripped off his clothes. He opened his arms and said, "Come here, baby."

Pam was mesmerized by the change in herself. She felt so right being here with him in the daylight. She loved him and was obviously giving him great pleasure. And he was sexy and handsome, and, she thought as she looked over his body, aroused. By me.

"Please, come here." He watched Pam rise. He took her in his arms and pressed his lips against hers. "Oh, darling, you feel good." He moved so her nipples brushed against the hair on his chest. "So good."

Pam ran her hands through his hair and pressed her mouth against his. When he touched the tip of his tongue to the inside of her mouth, she felt the shock waves ripple through her body.

"I don't want to play more poker to win your jeans and panties," Warren said, tearing his mouth away from hers. "Let's just say I win and you take them off."

She winked and said, "I guess I'm not very good at this game." She bent down and pulled off the rest of her clothes.

"You're going to be wonderful at all kinds of games I can think of."

Pam's eyes were glazed with newfound lust. "Now what?"

"Wait right here." Warren walked into the bathroom and returned with a large bath towel. "I wouldn't want you to get rug burn." He spread the towel in a sunny spot and said, "Lie here."

Gracefully, Pam sat down and lay back. Warren positioned her so that the sun shone on her belly and thighs. "Oh, sweetie, you look so lovely." He sat down beside Pam and kissed her full on the mouth while his hands roamed over her body. "Mmmm," he purred. "So lovely."

Pam felt the combined warmth of Warren's body and the sun shining on her skin. It was incredibly erotic and she felt her hunger grow.

Warren kissed her breasts and flicked his tongue over her nipples. "Your breasts taste so good," he whispered.

"Let me suck them." He suckled, first one breast, then the other. "So good."

"Oh, darling, it's you who feel so good."

When he could wait no longer, he insisted, "Tell me, baby. Tell me. Tell me you want me to make love to you." Would she say it? he wondered. Would she admit her sexuality out loud as she never had before? "Please tell me."

"Yes, Warren. Make love to me. I want you."

Quickly, Warren found a condom in his wallet and slipped it on. Then he thrust his erect cock into Pam's hot, wet body and, all too quickly, as he felt her come, he climaxed, too. He collapsed on top of her.

They must have dozed for a few minutes because the next thing Pam felt was pins and needles. "My leg is falling asleep," she said.

"Sorry," Warren said, rolling off of her, pulling her close. "That was terrific."

"It certainly was." She was thoughtful. "You know we never made love like this before."

"You mean on the living room floor in the middle of the afternoon?"

"I always thought that sex was supposed to happen in the bedroom, at night. This seems so decadent."

"And what's wrong with that?"

"Nothing. Nothing at all. I guess I have a lot to learn."

"I'll be glad to guide your education. And if you get too good at poker, we'll play different games. Lots of different games."

There are several points to Pam and Warren's story. First, sex is one of the most enjoyable activities there is. If it weren't, why would we devote so much time and thought to something that can be awkward, uncomfortable, and embarrassing?

Second, there's more to enjoyable sex than a quick fuck. Not that quickies are necessarily bad; it's just that there's so much more to making love than the actual insertion of a penis into a vagina. Foreplay is fun. And, although foreplay is usually a prelude to intercourse, it doesn't have to be a means to an end. It can be an end in itself.

Third, very small variations from basic lovemaking can enhance sex tremendously. Pam and Warren changed from the bedroom at night to the living room in the sunlight. But that small change ignited new and fierce feelings of lust.

The fourth, and maybe most important, point is that *anything two people agree to and that gives them both sexual pleasure is okay.*

As the author of books on sexual creativity, I have been asked, "Is good sex important to a long-lasting relationship." I now have a standard answer, one that is the theme of this book. "Let's take *important* out of sex and put *fun* back in." Everyone seems to be worried about their sex life. Don't worry—be happy. Silly for most situations, but so true for sex.

I often hear the same comments.

"Good sex is the cornerstone of our relationship, but our lovemaking is getting a little boring."

"I usually do for her. Sometimes, I want her to do for me."

"I don't think I climax soon enough to suit him."

"I don't think I'm big enough to suit her."

"I really don't like the way my body looks."

"I'm not too good in bed, and therefore I'll never have a good relationship."

"I'm really very good in bed. I've read all the books, studied all the erogenous zones, and I know how to give a woman an orgasm every time. I don't know why I can't build a lasting relationship. Women aren't able to keep up with me, I guess."

Let's put those last two comments to rest immediately. No one is "bad at sex" or "good in bed." Yes, there are people who are more willing to experiment, more receptive to another's needs and wishes, but no one is a "good lover." Good lovers exist only in pairs.

My partner, Ed, and I are good together. We experiment. We communicate. We tell each other what we enjoy and what we don't enjoy. We try new things, repeat some, and discard others. We play. Our sex life is fun. We look forward to spending sexual time together because it gives us each tremendous pleasure.

Another comment I hear about sex concerns one-upmanship.

"My wife and I had great sex last night and boy did I make out great. I got her to go down on me for the first time. I don't think she wanted to, but she owed it to me. After all . . ."

Hogwash. When sex becomes a contest—a power struggle, if you will—then no one wins. Everyone loses. The fun gets lost because each of the partners is keeping score. Making your partner do something that she doesn't want to do is bound to diminish her pleasure and will usually delay the next sexual encounter. Let's face it. If someone was making you do things you didn't want to do, wouldn't you put off the next unpleasant encounter as long as you could?

"But I want to try new things," I hear you saying. "How can I go about experimenting if you say I can't make my partner do new stuff?" The answer is simple: communication and temptation. As you will see, playing games is one way to tell your partner about the new and exciting things you would like to try.

There's an important reason to keep your sexual activities limited to one partner. In this "Age of AIDS," it is imperative that we all make the most of our monogamous relationships. Every new relationship increases the risk of getting a sexually transmitted disease. Of course, you can decrease that risk by practicing safe sex, using a condom at all times, as Warren did. But you can also minimize the risk by doing your playing at home with your full-time partner.

Here's another comment I frequently hear.

"My wife wouldn't be interested in anything off-center. She's too nice, too straight."

You may be right, but I doubt it. It's politically correct these days to put down sexual fantasies and off-center sex. It's considered improper to enjoy cavorting around the bedroom dressed up in silly outfits, acting out the parts in your favorite dream. Off-center is considered kinky and perverted, and those words have taken on sinister connotations. Most of this thinking refuses to differentiate between erotica, which depicts loving partners sharing fantasies, and pornography, which degrades and dehumanizes and may become violent and ugly.

While it's true that *she* may not be interested in dressing up like a hooker and prancing around the house with a whip in her hand, she might be interested in giving or getting a sensual massage. And whereas *he* might not want to be chained to the bed, he might want to let you call the shots and tell him exactly what to do to your body. Every tiny step forward and each successful experiment leads to others. Where you will end up . . . who knows?

So maybe you want to play, but you don't want to risk telling your partner about your desires.

"She'll think I'm kinky."

"He'll wonder where I got my off-center ideas."

"She won't want to get silly."

"He'll think I don't want him anymore."

"She wouldn't understand."

"He won't understand."

"Happily married people shouldn't feel this way."

Sexual communication is an especially risky and difficult skill for many of us, particularly those of us who learned little more than the missionary position when we were young. That's where bookmarking can help.

Here's what to do.

First, read this book slowly. Stop each time your juices get flowing and you want to make mad, passionate love to your partner. Do it. If the book does nothing more than stimulate nights of good sex, that's great. But there's a lot more.

When you reach a section of this book that intrigues you, put a bookmark in it. The section might contain a story you'd like to tell in the dark as a prelude to lovemaking or a fantasy you'd like to act out. You might find an activity you'd like to try, or even a new location or position for sex.

Now, here's the difficult part. Give the book to your partner—quickly, before you change your mind. Be brave. Sure it's risky, but the rewards are so marvelous.

Second, partner, you received this book from someone you care about. Read it with an open mind, and when you come to the bookmark, remember this: *Someone's trying to tell you something wonderful.* He's saying, "I want to play with *you,* not with anyone else." Or she's saying, "Share the fun and fantasy with me. Tell me that you'd enjoy the activity I've marked or move the bookmark to something you'd like to try instead. But let's communicate."

Maybe the section that your partner has bookmarked isn't your cup of tea. Maybe it's the last thing you've ever pictured yourself doing. That's okay. Move the bookmark. Select something else, something you think might be pleasurable, like an erotic massage or, like Warren, making love in the living room. Give the book back to your partner and wait. Hooray. You've just begun a dialogue.

Third, when you've selected something you'd both love to try, relax. You still may not have talked about it, but that's okay. You've communicated. Now, get into the evening. Since nothing ruins a good mood like being cold, turn the heat up. If you like and you don't have to drive later, have some whiskey, wine, or a beer. I suggest, however, that you use alcohol in moderation, because too much inhibits lovemaking. You don't want to fall asleep just when things are getting good.

Have a good supply of condoms on hand—for safe sex, contraception, for anal sex, or for the fun of the different feel of ribbed or prelubricated ones. Just have them; don't make value judgments. Be loose and open-minded.

Send the kids to the movies for the evening or ship them off to their grandparents' house for an overnight.

Let's take a moment to understand why you're getting rid of the kids. Contrary to what you're probably thinking, it's not so that they don't know what you're doing. When you feel they are old enough to understand, certainly before they are sexually active, teach your children that any consensual sex is okay. Help them to learn the difference between off-center sex between two consenting partners and date rape, forcing a partner to do something that she or he doesn't want to. Teach your children that no *always* means no.

So why are you getting rid of the children? For sex to be truly relaxed, you need privacy. Nothing ruins a good mood like a little voice asking, "Can I get into bed with you?" just at the wrong moment.

And realize that kids are usually more knowledgeable than we give them credit for. There's an old joke about a little eight-year-old boy who goes into the bathroom for a drink of water in the middle of the night. He stumbles upon his father putting on a condom. "Whatcha doin', Daddy?" the kid asks.

Totally flustered, the father answers with the first thing that comes into his mind. "I'm catching mice," he says.

"Gonna fuck 'em when ya catch 'em, Daddy?"

Enough said.

Fourth, don't get too exotic all at once. Start small, maybe with something simple like Warren and Pam did, or get into fantasies by playing Let's Tell Stories, described in Chapter 5.

You might want to play with some of the toys that are already around the house, like mirrors or water pistols. Or look through a catalog and imagine what some of the toys would feel like. If you feel adventurous, order something together. Whatever you do, play.

And forget about winners and losers. There are none. At the end of the movie *War Games,* the computer has figured out that in tic-tac-toe, if played correctly, no one ever wins. When it tries a war game, it states: "A strange game. The only winning move is not to play." With sex games, while it's true that there's some risk in playing, you always lose if you never play.

Fifth, whatever new activity you venture into, send warm, fuzzy messages to let your partner know that everything's okay. Purr, moan, use your body. If you're not enjoying whatever's happening, tell your partner that, too. Communicate. Sex must never become an endurance contest. But if you reject an idea, let your partner know that it's the idea you didn't enjoy, not your partner. He or she is not a bad person for suggesting something you didn't enjoy. Your partner took a great risk. Make it pay off by suggesting something different that you would enjoy.

There are some new ideas in this book. Others are merely new versions of old themes. If some of the ideas are repugnant to you, skip them and move on. There's something here for everyone.

If you don't want to play a new game but would like to begin by merely sharing a story with your partner instead, there are several bedtime stories in the chapter entitled "Let's Pretend" on page 109. Read silently together or read aloud.

If you don't find your favorite fantasy here, use the material in Chapter 5 to create your own story, mentioning a new sexual activity to your partner via an innocent reference in a story. Whatever the activity, mainstream or way off-center, check your partner's body language carefully to gauge his or her reaction. You may be pleasantly surprised.

Some of the "games" suggested in this book aren't games at all, just imaginative activities for the sexually active. Some are merely ways to suggest something new. Some stories depict activities that you may have been doing for a long time. Great.

Some ideas here may seem dumb to you. For example, you can't imagine yourself tied to a chair and being teased with a feather. Not your thing. Fine. But it's somebody's thing, I can assure you.

Just remember: Anything agreed upon by two consenting adults is okay.

"I get so embarrassed. What if I have to laugh or giggle?"

I get embarrassed, too, but, like Pam in the opening story, it's a delicious embarrassment. And if I have the urge to giggle, I do. Laughter is wonderful, even at the most intimate moments.

A few warnings before we begin. In this book, I use graphic language to describe lovemaking. I don't use clinical terms such as *vulva* and *penile insertion,* nor do I use euphemisms like *love nest* or *maleness.* Personally, I can't abide such phrases as, "He put his erect member into her hungry sex." So I use *cunt, cock, pussy,* and other common expressions.

By the way, if you've never used words like these, if

you've never said, "Please fuck me," or "I want to feel your hot cock deep inside my wet pussy," that can be exciting in and of itself. What's more, "forcing" your partner to say them during lovemaking can be very erotic.

Please note also that I use the words *he* and *she* interchangeably. Nothing suggested is a "male thing" or a "female thing." He may want to dress up as a male stripper or she may want to use a dildo on her partner's ass. Control can be given to either sex by the other. So I've been as open-minded about gender as possible. You should do likewise.

One last point. This book is not for people with serious sexual problems. If you are having difficulties that can't be *talked out* or if things are happening that you can't stop but don't enjoy, you may need help. Don't hesitate to seek professional assistance.

Okay. Now that we've agreed on the basics, it's time to begin playing games and using toys.

Turn the page and come play with me.

1

LET'S PLAY FOR FORFEITS

Why play games? People play for fun, to experiment and to communicate.

You may have already seen or played some of the computer sex games on the market. One of the first and possibly the most famous is Leisure Suit Larry, an adventure-type game in which Larry tries and tries to get laid. At one point, when he has finally gotten into bed with a prostitute, if he doesn't use a condom, he contracts a serious disease and dies. I've never actually seen it, but I'm told that when you type in "Fuck you," the machine tells you, "You can't do that . . . yet." Sex games are here to stay.

So you might want to play a game. A first step might be to play a common game for a forfeit, as Pam and Warren did. So let's start there.

There are many ways to use forfeits. Use them to suggest an activity you've always wanted to try or to encourage your partner to communicate with you. Suggest what you want "in jest," but remember that many a truth is spoken in jest. If your partner mentions something, then backs away, saying, "Just kidding," use your antennae. Maybe he or she is suggesting something you both might enjoy.

Forfeits can be used to play control games. As your partner's forfeit, you can insist that he be your slave for an hour, then "force" him to do some of the things you've always wanted. Or make him lie still while you do things to his "helpless" body. These are common control fantasies that can be translated into games. They're so common and exist in so many forms that I've saved control games for an entirely separate chapter.

For now, let's see what happened to a few people who used forfeits to embark on new adventures.

FRAN AND MARK'S STORY

Fran and her husband, Mark, had been playing Yahtzee for forfeits for a few months. As a matter of fact, it had become a Friday-night ritual. Once their teenaged daughter had left for her job at the mall and their son had gone to his basketball game, they took out the dice and played six games. After six games, the one with fewer total points owed the winner a forfeit.

Over the months, they had ventured into a number of only slightly off-center areas. Fran had enjoyed evenings of being rubbed with body lotion and, one particularly

interesting evening, of having Mark wait on her for an
hour. Mark, on the other hand, had finally been brave
enough to ask Fran to touch his cock, and, much to
Fran's surprise, she had learned that she enjoyed giving
her husband pleasure in this way.

This evening, when Mark, the official scorekeeper,
added the points, the six-game tournament had ended in
a tie. "One game," he said with a smirk. "Winner takes
all."

Thanks to a lucky throw of five sixes, Mark won. "I want
to take my forfeit differently tonight," he said. "I want to
lie in bed, cuddle, and make love leisurely. Then, at some
moment, I'll pick a forfeit and tell you what it will be.
Okay?"

"Sure," Fran said. "You're tonight's big winner."

Fran and Mark cleaned up the remains of their game,
put the front porch light on for the kids, and took their
wineglasses and the remaining quarter of a bottle up to
the bedroom. Fran washed up and changed into her
most revealing nightgown while Mark brushed his teeth,
stripped down, and put on a pair of pajama bottoms, all
he ever wore to bed.

Mark and his wife climbed into bed and flipped on the
TV. "How about a little Playboy Channel to warm up?"
Mark asked. Fran pressed the appropriate numbers on
the remote control and a video of a man kneeling between a woman's legs, licking her pussy with long, wet
strokes, appeared. The camera was alternately focusing
on her face and his mouth.

"You know in these movies, the woman never looks like
she's having any fun," Mark said. "She just looks bored.
But he seems to be having fun." Mark could feel himself

getting hard. He'd love to do that to Fran, but he didn't think she'd enjoy it. Maybe he could use his forfeit. . . .

After some inane conversation and scene switching, the picture changed. Now, a man was fucking a woman from behind. He wasn't fucking her in the anus. Rather, his penis was lodged firmly in the woman's cunt, but he had entered her from behind, curled against her back spoon-fashion. Mark's body reacted immediately. That position seemed so tame in comparison with some of the more outlandish things people did in those movies, but making love to his wife that way had been a secret dream of his for a long time. It seemed so animal-like somehow. But he wanted it. Could he use his forfeit?

They watched the movie for a while, both getting hotter and hotter. "I really like these ridiculous movies," Fran said. "They're so predictable and they have no story to speak of, but watching people fuck always gets my juices flowing."

"I don't know how those guys do it," Mark said, trying to make conversation while working up the nerve to ask for what he wanted. "I couldn't get an erection with three dozen technicians watching."

"Maybe that's why they use the same few guys over and over," Fran said. "Women, on the other hand, can get turned on or not; it doesn't matter. A little lubricant, if necessary, and shazaam." She snuggled closer to Mark's body. "Me, I get turned on just thinking about making love with you."

While the movie played in the background, Mark nuzzled Fran's neck and nibbled on the tender skin where her shoulder joined her neck. "You're delicious," he said.

Mark nibbled a line up Fran's neck until he reached

her ear. He licked the lobe, then sucked it into his mouth. He felt Fran's body react to the gentle suction. "Mmm," he purred, "you taste so good."

He released the pressure and then alternately licked the inside of Fran's ear and nipped on her earlobe. He slid his hand up Fran's rib cage and circled her lace-covered breast with the tip of his finger. "Oh, baby," he said. He pulled himself up on one elbow and nibbled his way along Fran's jawline toward her mouth. As Mark's fingers teased his wife's breast, his lips teased her mouth. He took his time, feeling his wife's heat increase.

When he felt her body writhe with need, he tightened his fingers and pinched her tight nipple. "Oh God," she said, "you make me so hot." She rubbed her hip against Mark's hard cock, which was pressed against her side. "I want you so much. Fuck me good."

He was going to do it. "I want my forfeit now," Mark said. "Something I've always wanted but never have been able to ask for."

Fran's ears perked up. "Tell me," she whispered. "Tell me, baby. Please tell me how to make you happy."

Without a word, he turned her body away from him and slid her nightgown up to her waist. "I want you this way." He rubbed his hard cock against the cleavage between her buttocks.

Fran sighed. "I don't think I'm ready for ass-fucking," she said, sorry that she couldn't do what he wanted. But she really wasn't ready for anal sex, even for Mark.

"That's not what I had in mind. Trust me, baby. Please."

Fran's body relaxed. She did trust her husband—completely. He would never do anything to hurt her and he would always stop if she asked. "It's your forfeit," she purred. "I am your dutiful slave."

Mark slid his cock into the cleft between Fran's thighs and felt her wetness. He didn't remember ever being so excited. He was really going to do it. He had fantasized about making love to his wife this way for so long.

He reached down and wrapped his hand around his cock. Slowly, so slowly, he rubbed it in and out of the cleft, feeling her juices wet his penis. "Curl up," he growled, "and let me fuck you this way."

Fran pulled her knees up toward her chest and arched her back. She felt the tip of Mark's cock against her opening. "Oh yes, baby," she purred, "do it. Do it now."

Mark rammed his erection deep into Fran's pussy and took her breast in his hand. Kneading her tit and nipping at her neck, he hammered into her until he came, smothering his scream against her back.

Mark had climaxed, but Fran wasn't satisfied. Her body was hot and hungry, and she knew exactly what she wanted. Now that Mark had taken the risk and asked for what he wanted, she would do the same. As she lay pressed against her husband, she knew she couldn't voice her desires, but she could ask another way.

A few moments later, as his breathing calmed, Mark felt Fran's hand take his and slide it around her body and between her legs. "I need you," she murmured.

"Oh yes, baby," Mark said, rubbing her clit. "Don't move." As he rubbed her clit with his semi-erect penis still inside of her, he felt her body show him the rhythm she wanted. He drew Fran's earlobe into his mouth and sucked in the same rhythm as his finger was using on her clit.

"Just like that," she said, her breathing rapid and shallow. "Don't stop. I'm going to come." Without moving her hips, she let her orgasm flow down her channel and felt it squeeze Mark's cock.

"Oh, darling," Mark said. "I've never felt anything like this." His cock was being massaged with waves of muscle contractions. Since his body was satisfied, he could lie still and feel his wife's climax. It seemed to go on for minutes.

When they had both calmed, Mark slowly withdrew his penis from Fran's body and held her close. "That was sensational," he whispered.

"Ummmm" was Fran's only response. She hesitated, then asked, "Was fucking me from behind something you had wanted for a long time?"

Mark was so embarrassed, he could only nod.

"You feel good fucking me that way," Fran said, remembering her climax, "and you were so hot." She swallowed hard. "And I wanted you to touch me. It was so good when you stroked me. It's too bad it's taken so long for us to find new things we enjoy."

"Yeah, it sure is. I didn't expect it to be so easy."

"Me, neither. Are there any other *evil* ideas lurking in the back of that brain of yours?" The way she purred the word *evil* made Mark's penis jerk.

"Well . . ." he grinned. "But they're so hard to talk about."

"Well, we'll just have to act some of them out, won't we? Maybe I'll use my next forfeit to *convince* you to do something truly evil to me."

Mark grinned. "Yeah, maybe."

CONNIE AND SCOTT'S STORY

"I don't believe this," Scott said as he added up the value of the cards left in his hand. "You've had the most amazing luck tonight."

"Not luck," his wife, Connie, said with a laugh, "skill. So what's the damage?"

"Another fifty-three points." He calculated the final score on the pad next to his beer glass. "At ten cents a point, the total is . . ."

"Yessss?"

"I owe you three-hundred seventy-two dollars and sixty cents."

"Wow. That's the most I've won in any evening since we've been playing. Maybe I'll just take it out in trade." Connie winked.

"What?" Suddenly Scott perked up. "Like what kind of trade?"

"I was just joking, dear," Connie said. "Just add my winnings to our running score and let's get to bed."

"Not so fast," Scott said. Connie had a kind of sexy glint in her eye he hadn't seen in quite a while. "Like what kind of trade?"

"Oh, it's nothing. I was just thinking . . ."

"Come on. I owe you a fortune just for tonight. Why don't you give me a chance to work it off?"

"I'd love a hot bath. Maybe you could work off the debt by running one for me, bath salts and all."

"How much would a bath be worth?" Scott asked, his mind whirling furiously. Since Melissa's birth, their sex life had been very quiet. Here was an opportunity for some old-fashioned fun, and he didn't intend to let it get away.

"Let's say one hundred dollars."

"And for another hundred, I'll clean up after our game and do the dishes."

"Done."

"And don't move until I'm ready."

"But I've got to check on the baby."

"Okay, check on the baby, then meet me in the bathroom."

Scott got up, rinsed the plates and glasses left over from their late dinner, and put them in the dishwasher. Then he started the hot water running in the big double tub in the bathroom and added two scoops of his wife's favorite lavender bath salts. He took the space heater from the bathroom closet and turned it on to heat the room.

As the tub filled, Scott pulled off his sneakers and socks, then his sweatshirt and sweatpants. Dressed only in his jockey shorts, he called, "You almost ready?"

"Coming." The bathroom door opened and Connie came in wearing her slinkiest negligee. "Baby's sound asleep." She put the portable receiver from the baby's intercom system on the bathroom counter. "That bath looks wonderful." She looked her husband's body over. "You do, too."

Scott reached for her. "Forget the bath, gorgeous, and let's go into the bedroom."

Connie squirmed away. "Not on your life. You owe me a bath and I intend to collect. Did you load the dishwasher?"

"Sure did. Let's see." Scott calculated. "That reduces my indebtedness to one hundred seventy-two sixty."

Connie dropped her negligee and stepped, beautifully naked, into the sudsy water. "Wonderful!" She sighed as she sank into the tub. "Now, for ten dollars, rub my neck."

Scott bent over the back of the tub and touched his wife's shoulders. "Yipes," she yelped. "Your hands are freezing. Soak them in the hot water and get them warm first." Dutifully, Scott dipped his hands into the water but, under the bubbles, he laid his palm on Connie's stomach.

"Not fair," she squealed. Playfully, she sprayed water in his face.

"Okay, okay," Scott said. He soaked his hands until the skin was warm, then began to knead Connie's shoulders. Digging his thumbs into the muscles of her upper back, he felt her relax.

"That's wonderful," she said. "Rub lower down my back."

"Another ten bucks." When she nodded, he said, "Lean forward." As he felt her respond, Scott slid his soapy hands lower, into the small of her back, under the water.

"Yeah, that's good."

"For another hundred dollars of the debt I owe you, I'll give you an all-over dry-down."

Connie saw the lust on his face and quickly agreed. She swiftly soaped her body, used the hand-held shower spray to rinse herself, stood up, and stepped, dripping, out of the tub. "Okay. Dry me off."

Scott took a thick bath towel from the rod and leisurely

rubbed it over Connie's body. Then he blew a stream of cool air over one breast and watched her nipple contract. "Not fair." She giggled.

"Who said anything about fair?" He grabbed her around the waist. "Turn around." Instead of the bath towel, he reached for a small facecloth and rubbed it over Connie's back. Then he slid the cloth up the backs of her thighs and between her cheeks. Up and down, he massaged that tender area. He watched as Connie's head fell back and her breathing deepened.

He used his tongue to lick one last drop of water from the small of his wife's back, then said, "Now turn around."

Scott squatted and rubbed the cloth over the instep of Connie's right foot. Then he carefully ran the cloth between each toe. Connie giggled and grabbed the towel rod. "That tickles."

Scott stood up and folded the big bath towel on the edge of the tub. "Sit down."

Naked, Connie sat on the edge of the tub and Scott sat on the fluffy bath mat. "Are you warm enough?" he asked. Connie glanced at the heater and smiled. "Warm as toast."

"Good." He again lifted her right foot and resumed drying it, pressing just hard enough so that it wouldn't tickle. When he was done, he said, "Now the other."

"But it's dry now," Connie said.

Scott lifted her left foot and put her big toe in his mouth. He sucked her toe, drawing on it as though he were suckling one of her nipples. "Now it's wet again."

For long, luxurious minutes, he alternately wet a toe and dried it. As he shifted back to her right foot, Connie was amazed how wet her pussy was becoming. "That's so sexy, Scott."

Scott put her foot down and rubbed the facecloth up the inside of her lower leg and across the back of her knee. His eyes were on his wife's face, watching the pleasure so obvious there.

With feather-soft strokes, he dusted the cloth back and forth over the backs of Connie's knees. "Oh, honey," he purred, "does that feel good?"

"It feels wonderful. Don't stop."

"Another hundred off my debt?"

"You drive a hard bargain." She looked down at her husband's erection, large and hard between his thighs, and grinned. "Very hard indeed."

"Deal?"

"Deal."

Slowly, he stroked the cloth up the insides of Connie's thighs, then back toward her knees. He bent over and licked the tender flesh inside her right thigh, then blew on the wet spot. Before Connie could react, he dried the area, only to do the same thing to the inside of her left leg.

"This one's free of charge," he said as he leaned forward and suckled her nipple. As he had with her thighs, he alternately licked and suckled her nipple, blew on the moist skin, then dried it off with light strokes of the facecloth. He repeated his ministrations on her other breast.

"Oh, Scott," she purred, "you make me so hot. Let's go into the bedroom and finish this right."

"Not so fast," Scott said. "I'm not done." He looked down. "You're not dry yet . . . all over. Spread your legs so I can dry you thoroughly."

Connie looked puzzled, then grinned. She dutifully separated her knees. When he said, "Wider," she obliged, opening herself to him.

"Now, as I was doing." Scott softly brushed the cloth over the hot flesh on her upper thighs, then over her pussy lips. He leaned forward, stuck his tongue out, and flicked the tip over Connie's clit. "Oh God," she said. "I'm so hot that if you do that, I'll come right here."

"And if I stop?"

"I'll fall apart. Don't stop."

"Another hundred."

Continuing with the pretense of his indebtedness to her, Connie nodded. "Oh yes, do it."

With long strokes of his tongue, Scott licked Connie's pussy. Then he licked at the inside of her inner lips and slowly swirled his tongue deep inside. He pulled out and drove in again. Over and over, he licked her clit, then fucked her cunt with his tongue. He felt the juices flow from her body, and, suddenly, she reached down and pressed his mouth firmly against her cunt. "Yes . . ." she screamed as she came. "That's so good."

As Connie sat on the edge of the tub with her husband's arms around her waist and his head resting in her lap, it took several minutes for her body to calm down. "Wow. That was sensational."

"It sure was."

Connie looked down at Scott's hard cock. "But you haven't come yet," she said.

Scott sat back on his haunches and silently ticked off some numbers on his fingers. "Let's see. You spent twenty dollars on a back rub, one hundred on a dry-down, and there were two one-hundred-dollar 'Don't stop's.' That's three hundred and twenty dollars. As I calculate this," he said, "you now owe me roughly one hundred and fifty bucks."

Connie thought a moment, then smiled and nodded. "That's about right. Got any ideas about how I could work off my debt?"

"Lots, my dear. I have lots of wonderful ideas."

JIM AND CHRISTY'S STORY

"Pennsylvania Avenue with a hotel. That's fourteen hundred dollars you owe me." Jim looked across the Monopoly board at his wife. "Come on, pay up. Pay up."

Christy counted her money. "I only have two hundred and seventy-five. I can sell the houses I have left on my Orange properties, but those are my only chance to get back in the game." She shrugged. "I guess the game's over." Reluctantly, she started to put her few remaining bills back into the game's box.

"Wait, wait. I'll give you a chance to catch up. Five hundred dollars a garment. We can call it strip Monopoly."

Christy and Jim had an active and creative sex life and they had occasionally played strip poker as a prelude to lovemaking, but not recently. Lately, things had been somewhat tame. Jim realized that this was a good time to spice things up again.

Christy thought about their two young children, both heavy sleepers, and realized they probably wouldn't be disturbed. Strip Monopoly. Sounds like a great start for a fun evening.

"Five hundred dollars for each thing I'm wearing?"

"Same rules as always," Jim said, removing his shoes, socks, and wristwatch. "Only actual clothes count."

"Make it one piece of clothing per fine and it's a deal." Christy saw her husband nod. She quickly removed her tennis shoes, socks, and her watch. With a wink, Christy pulled her sweater off over her head. As usual, Jim enjoyed the sight of his wife's ample breasts filling her bra.

"All right." Christy laughed. "That pays me up for now. Stop ogling and throw the dice."

The game progressed for a while, then Christy landed on Chance and drew a card. "Advance to Illinois Avenue," she read. "That's yours, and with a hotel."

"Eleven hundred dollars. Got any money?"

"Not enough," Christy said, a slow smile spreading across her face. "Got any other ideas?"

"Your bra."

She wasn't going to make this too easy. The fun was in the anticipation. "Settle for my jeans and you've got a deal."

"Is this a negotiation?" Jim asked.

"Take my jeans, or we have to end the game."

"Okay, I'll take the jeans."

During the next few rounds, it looked like the tide was turning. Christy collected a few rents, but then she landed in jail. On her next throw, however, she got out of jail and then again landed on Illinois Avenue. Without asking, Christy stood up, reached behind her, and unsnapped her bra. With exaggerated thrusting of her breasts, she removed the tiny garment and handed it to her husband. Wearing only brief bikini panties, she sat back down and handed the dice to Jim.

As the game progressed, Christy deliberately spent any rent money she collected on houses and hotels so that, if she landed on any of Jim's properties, she'd be broke. She knew a good idea when she saw one, so winning the game was the furthest thing from her mind.

Fortunately for both players, Christy's bad luck continued. Soon her panties joined her bra. Now totally naked, she said, "I wonder what happens if I land on any other of your properties now."

A few throws later, Jim landed on one of Christy's hotels and Christy refused money. "I want your sweatshirt instead." Jim agreed and quickly removed his shirt.

As they played, the sexual tension increased. Jim frequently shifted his position to ease the pressure in his jeans and Christy sat with her legs curled under her to keep her wet body away from the sofa she was sitting on.

Christy threw the dice and advanced her tiny shoe marker around the board. Jim grinned as her marker stopped. "That's St. Charles Place. Seven hundred and fifty dollars," Jim said, "and you seem to be out of clothes. I need to figure out a suitable forfeit." How did that thought escape his mouth? He'd been thinking it, but suddenly it was said.

"Forfeit?" Christy was amazed and delighted at her husband's creativity. She'd certainly go along, and she let her expression show her willingness. "Like what?"

"I'll pour you a soda while I try to think of something suitable."

Quickly, Christy got up and boosted the thermostat. As she heard the heat come on, she sat back on the sofa and looked at the Monopoly board on the coffee table. For-feits, she thought. How delicious. It opened so many pos-sibilities.

As he poured soda into two glasses, Jim thought about the forfeit. He could be real tame and have her give him a back rub or kiss him. He could even have her suck his cock, something he'd always wanted. As he thought, he realized that now he had the opportunity to ask for things he'd always wanted. But did he dare?

He walked back into the living room and saw Christy stretched out on the sofa. "Come on," she said, making it obvious with her voice and her body language that she was willing to go along with whatever Jim suggested.

Jim sat on the end of the sofa near his wife's feet and set the two glasses on the coffee table. "I've decided on your forfeit," he said, his voice husky. "I want to watch you touch yourself."

She had expected a variety of things, but not this. She didn't know that watching her was something that would give Jim pleasure. Christy raised an eyebrow and adjusted her body so Jim could see her wet pussy. She slid her fin-gers downward through her pubic hair. "You mean like this?"

Jim merely nodded. Slowly, Christy moved her fingers over her wet, swollen flesh, her eyes never leaving her husband's face. He had a look of pure bliss in his eyes that she'd seen only a few times before. One more way to give him pleasure, she realized, and not only now but at other times.

Jim watched and shuddered. Then he cleared his throat. "That's enough," he said. He turned back to the board. "My turn."

He threw the dice and landed on Chance. "You've been elected chairman of the board. Pay each player fifty dollars." He started to count out the cash.

"I don't want the money. I want your jeans instead."

"Hmmm. Fifty-dollar jeans." After a moment's pause, Jim stood up and pulled off his jeans, trying to hide the huge bulge in his jockey shorts.

Money forgotten, the game continued. Soon, Jim had lost his shorts and sat on the sofa naked and obviously excited. This time, it was Jim's luck to land on one of Christy's properties with a hotel. The subject of money didn't even come up.

"You owe me a forfeit," Christy said. "And I believe your idea will work for me, too."

"My idea?"

"I want to watch you touch yourself."

Jim's face turned beet red. "You what?"

"I want to watch you touch yourself. You wanted to watch me, and I could tell by your face that it was a turn-on. Now I want the same pleasure."

"It never occurred to me that you would want something like that."

"Me, neither," Christy said with a smile, "but you're stalling. Wrap your hand around your cock and run your hand up and down."

Jim's hands were shaking. "I'm really embarrassed."

"I know. I was, too. But that's part of the fun. I'm assuming that yours is the sexy kind of embarrassment that I felt."

Jim grinned. "I guess it is." Tentatively, he wrapped his hands around his erect cock and lightly slid his hand toward the tip. He tried not to enjoy the feeling too much, but he was very aroused. He closed his eyes and flowed with the wonderful sensations.

After a few moments, Christy realized that Jim was so excited that he might climax at any moment. "Not yet," she said. "Stop what you're doing right now."

Jim dropped his hand, a guilty expression on his face.

"Sometime, I want to watch you do that until you come," Christy said. "But not right now." She threw the dice and, to her delight, landed on Illinois Avenue yet again. "Let's make this for one last forfeit, this time in the bedroom." She blew him a kiss. "Think carefully about what you want. I'm game for anything."

While they cleaned up the game, Jim thought about the forfeit. He knew what he wanted. All he had to do was ask. Together, they gathered their clothes and walked upstairs.

In the bedroom, Christy stretched out on the bed, gloriously naked. She knew Jim was hesitating. There was something he wanted to ask for, but it was so hard for him to make the suggestion.

"I can tell from your face that you're thinking about something wonderfully naughty," Christy said. "I'd love to know what it is."

"It's hard for me to talk about some things."

"Please . . ."

"I want to watch you use your vibrator to make yourself come."

Christy was flabbergasted but delighted. "I'd love to do that for you, if that's what you want. Would you stroke yourself at the same time so I can watch?"

Words wouldn't come out of Jim's mouth, so he merely nodded. Christy reached into the back of her bedside table drawer and found the plastic case. They had bought the vibrator from a catalog a few years earlier, then played with it a few times while they made love. Recently, it had gathered dust in the back of Christy's drawer. Christy plugged the toy in and flipped the switch. The familiar hum filled the room. She flicked it off again.

Christy put one leg on each side of Jim so he could get a good look at her pussy, reached down between her legs, and used her fingers to spread her juices around slowly. "I have to get my body very wet so the vibrator will slide around." She had to do no such thing, but she was enjoying watching Jim's eyes fixed on her fingers.

"I'm so wet," she purred. "I guess it's time for the show now." She turned the vibrator on and slowly slid the tip through her pubic hair. "Don't forget. You have to touch your big hard cock for me," she murmured.

As Jim watched the vibrator slip between his wife's legs, he wrapped his hand around his engorged cock and began to stroke himself. He knew that he wouldn't be able to hold back for long, and suddenly, embarrassing as it was, he wanted Christy to see him come all over his hand.

As Christy watched the look of bliss spread over her husband's face, she relaxed and let the vibrator touch her clit. It took only seconds before she felt the familiar tightening in her belly. "I'm going to come," she cried. "Right *now*." Waves of orgasm washed over her and she flipped the machine off. She opened her eyes and saw Jim stroking his rigid penis.

Suddenly, he yelled, "Oh yes, baby. Oh yes." Semen spurted from the tip of his penis, wetting his hand and thighs. "Oh God," he said as he collapsed on the bed next to Christy. "So good."

Christy reached over and grabbed a handful of tissues. Gently, she wiped the gooey liquid from Jim's body, then used another wad of tissues to clean up her own juices.

"I don't believe how good that was." Jim sighed.

Christy was silent. "What are you thinking?" Jim said, wondering whether she now regretted the game.

Christy laughed. "Actually, I was wondering whether we could play strip backgammon."

2

LET'S PLAY A FEW BASIC GAMES

Are these games silly? Of course. Are they fun? Absolutely. After reading the stories that follow, some of you may choose to play one of these games, or you may prefer to invent games of your own. Some of you will decide that game playing isn't your thing because, for you, it feels artificial and awkward. But as you read, I'm sure you will find new and different sexual avenues to explore, because imbedded within these games are ideas that will excite even the most traditional lover.

I suggest you have a bookmark handy. Maybe you'll be turned on by a particular game, or just a position, place, or time of day. Whatever strikes you, mark it quickly, before you censor your thoughts and reject what might be a delightful possibility.

LET'S PLAY BLINDMAN'S BUFF

Barb read about the game in a woman's magazine article. "Spice Up Your Sex Life with Games" was the title of the article, and the game, which dealt with blindfolds, seemed like a deliciously erotic idea. Being blindfolded, then touched and caressed had always intrigued her and was part of an old fantasy. Now that she and Kevin occasionally bookmarked an article or story, she had a way to indicate to him that she would like to play. She used a yellow Hi-Liter to mark the section of the article called "Blindman's Buff," then bookmarked the article and put the magazine on Kevin's bedside table.

That evening, Barb volunteered to put their seven-month-old daughter, Penny, in her crib for the night and suggested that Kevin relax on the bed. He hurried down the hall and into the bedroom. He knew the signs. Barb had found a new game.

Kevin climbed onto their bed and spotted the magazine on the table next to him, its bookmark peeking out from between the pages. It's amazing, he thought. Just knowing that Barb has suggested something new makes me so horny. I wonder what she's telling me now.

He opened the magazine to the marked page, found the yellow marks, and read. When he finished the story, he sat back. Blindfolds. He had never really thought about being deprived of sight before, but, as he considered the idea, it seemed that other senses might be enhanced. An interesting concept, he thought. I wonder whether Barb wants to be blindfolded or whether she

wants to blindfold me? Kevin rummaged around in a few
bureau drawers before he found a wide soft silk scarf that
could be used to cover someone's eyes.

A while later, he heard Barb come down the hall from
Penny's room. As she walked into the bedroom, Kevin
asked, "Want to play Blindman's Buff, Barb?"

"Sure," she said, suddenly breathless. "Could I be *it*?"

It, he remembered from the story, was the person who
was blindfolded. Barb wanted to be blindfolded. "Okay.
I'll blindfold you and you can try to find me. You get one
minute. If you haven't found me by then, I'll say something, then give you another minute. If you find me, then
I have to pay a penalty. If not"—he leered and twirled his
nonexistent mustache—"then your blindfolded body is
mine."

Without another word, Barb walked up to Kevin and
turned her back. Quickly, he tied the scarf across her
eyes and spun her around a few times. Then, as quietly as
he could, he climbed onto the king-sized bed and stood
in the very center.

"I'm very dizzy," she said. Kevin was silent. She waited
for a moment and then, when Kevin didn't say anything,
she said, "No good trying to get you to say anything, I
guess." With her arms extended in front of her and her
legs moving slowly to feel her way around the room, she
searched for her husband. "Where are you?" she said,
hoping that he wouldn't reveal himself. "You can move
around, you know, but I might hear you."

As the first minute passed and she was unable to find
her husband, she became frustrated. She had become so
involved in the competition that she had momentarily
forgotten that she wanted to lose.

Kevin eased himself to the far side of the bed and said, "One minute."

"You're over there," Barb said, turning toward the sound. "I've got you now." She felt her way to the other side of the room, but, by the time she got there, Kevin had silently climbed back into the center of the big bed. "Where the hell are you?" Barb said, her frustration increasing.

"You'll never know," Kevin said, moving toward the far side of bed.

Barb continued to search but couldn't locate her husband.

Kevin climbed off the far side of the bed. "That's your second minute," he said, looking at his watch. "Your time is up."

Barb pulled up her blindfold and there, on the other side of the bed, was her husband, grinning at her.

"Where were you?" she asked.

"That's for me to know and you to think about for the next time we play." He smiled. "But now, you're mine. Strip."

She was acting out an old fantasy of hers and it made her a bit uncomfortable to be so close to something she had previously only dreamed about. Sensing her momentary discomfort, Kevin said, "Come on now, gorgeous. Remove the rest of those clothes."

Barb hesitated, then realized that it was okay. As a matter of fact, it was fantastic.

When she was naked, she allowed Kevin to pull her onto the bed and tie the blindfold back into place. Barb took a deep, calming breath and forced her body to relax.

With the blindfold covering her eyes and heightening her senses, Barb concentrated on the feeling of Kevin's hand stroking her breasts and pinching her nipples. She felt her nipples harden as she spread her legs wider apart. She wanted him—a lot.

Kevin stopped, no longer touching her. "What shall I do now?" Barb was puzzled. Wasn't he going to touch her between her spread legs, where she ached to be touched? Softly, Kevin said, "I asked you a question. What shall I do now?"

"What do you mean?"

"Well, you're mine now and I intend to make the most of it. I've always wanted to hear you tell me exactly what you want, so speak to me. Tell me what to do next, step by step. In clear four-letter words."

Barb lay spread-eagled on the bed, wet and hot. Deprived of her sight, she found Kevin's voice sounded unusually loud. She wanted him to touch her very much, but what could she say? "I don't know. Do whatever you want."

"I'll give you several choices this time, but from here on, you'll have to tell me, in detail, exactly what you want. So, to start, your choices are as follows. I will either fuck you right now, or lick your pussy, or maybe you would like to suck my cock?"

The words Kevin was using shot through Barb's body like electricity. Kevin occasionally used words like those in the heat of passion. She remembered times when he had said things like, "I love fucking you," or "You have such a beautiful pussy." But he had never said anything like this during foreplay. And she never used words like that at all. So what could she say? "All of them, I guess," she whispered. God, she wanted to feel his mouth on her, but she couldn't possibly bring herself to say it.

"That's the wrong answer, darling. I gave you three choices and you have to pick one."

She drew a deep breath. "I want you to put your mouth on me." There, she'd said it.

"That wasn't one of the choices. If that's what you want, you have to say, 'I want you to lick my pussy.' Get it?"

"I can't say those words," Barb said, getting hotter and more frustrated by the moment. She raised her hand to remove the blindfold, to show him her frustration by the look she usually gave him.

As Kevin carefully watched his wife's body language, he realized how hot the words were making her. He also suspected that she didn't want him to stop, so he pushed her hand away. "Leave the blindfold alone and do as you're told." He pressed on. "You have no choice. You lost the game and you're mine. Say, 'I want you to lick my pussy.' "

Somehow, deep inside, she wanted to be forced to use that kind of language. She felt Kevin's knuckle brush her pubic hair. She wanted him so much. "I want you to lick me."

" 'Lick my pussy.' Say it."

"I want you to lick my pussy." She was so excited that with the words she was saying, the blindfold, and the feeling of the flat of Kevin's tongue now making long, soft strokes across her vagina, she was close to climax. She tried to push herself over the edge, but as Kevin licked and sucked, he seemed to know just how to keep her on the brink of orgasm without letting her come.

"Now what do you want?" he asked, his tongue now still.

"Oh God," she moaned. "Be inside of me. I need you." She felt so empty. She needed to be filled and she needed to come.

"I know it's hard for you to say the words, but you have to." When she hesitated, he said, "Okay. I'll tell you what you want, then you say it. Say, 'I want you to finger-fuck my pussy.' " When Barb hesitated, Kevin tickled her cunt and flicked her clit with his tongue. Then he drew back and blew a cool stream of air across her wet body. "Say it," he said again.

"I want you to . . ."

" 'Finger-fuck my pussy.' " He finished the sentence for her. "Say it."

"I want you to finger-fuck my pussy."

Kevin quickly inserted first one, then two fingers into Barb's cunt and rubbed in and out. He stroked her inner walls and rubbed her lips and clit. When he felt her getting close to orgasm, he stopped. "I don't want you to come yet, dear. Not until you ask me to let you come while I finger-fuck your cunt."

"Please," Barb said, her breathing rapid and her body squirming. With the blindfold still in place, she could only hear and feel.

"Say, 'Please let me come while you finger-fuck my cunt and lick my clit.' You've got to ask me for everything exactly." He pulled his fingers out of her body and softly stroked the insides of her thighs.

She needed him so much and the words were so exciting that she said them with only a moment's hesitation.

"Let me come. Finger-fuck my cunt and lick my clit. Please."

"You're such a good girl that I'll do exactly what you want." He fucked her cunt with three fingers while he flicked the tip of his tongue over her clit. "Come now, baby," he said between licks. "Come for me."

And she did, moaning, "Sooo good. Sooo very good."

He pulled his fingers out, unzipped his pants, and pulled out his cock. Still clothed, he plunged into Barb's body and fucked her hard. "Yes, darling, so wonderful." He continued to push in and pull out until he could wait no longer. "Yes, darling, I love fucking your cunt." He felt her body clench against his. "I'm going to come inside you," he said loudly. Kevin felt semen spurt deep into Barb's body as he tightened his buttocks and pressed his body hard against hers. "Oh yes," he said again. "Oh yes."

Later, he said, "That was so good, baby. It makes me crazy to watch your body lose control as you come." He pulled off her blindfold and kissed her eyes. "Next time, I want to watch your eyes while you say all those terribly naughty things you said."

"Next time?"

"Many next times."

Playing games was not new to Maggie and Herb. They had learned to keep an open mind and listen to any new game suggestion. They also felt free to reject an idea that didn't sound like fun and substitute another one. This particular evening, it was Herb who had the idea. All the way home from work, he had been turning the game over in his mind, improving on his original idea until he knew exactly how he wanted to play.

LET'S PLAY PEEKABOO

"Let's play a game," Herb said to his wife, Maggie, after dinner.

Maggie loved it when her husband suggested game playing. It always meant that an evening of unusual sex would follow. "Exactly what did you have in mind?" She wondered whether he wanted to play an old favorite or had invented something new.

"I had an idea driving home from work and it's had me hot ever since."

"Rules?"

"Take off all of your clothes, then lie down on the bed, faceup. Once the game begins, I don't want you to move." When she looked at him quizzically, he said, "It's my game and I get to play tonight."

"Okay, maestro. It's your concerto." Maggie pulled off her sneakers and socks, then stripped off her jeans, sweater, and undies. She lay down on the bed and looked at Herb. "What's that?" she asked, looking at the piece of old bed sheet he had put on the end of the bed.

"You'll see." He set a feathery long frond from the artificial flower arrangement in the dining room on the bedside table and put his ice-filled soda glass next to it. Then he went into the kitchen and returned with the timer they used during the word games they often played. It could be set for from thirty seconds to ten minutes and made a bell-like sound when time expired.

"Now, here's how this is going to work. I'm going to put this sheet over you." He stretched the sheet over the full length of Maggie's body. "Does having the sheet over your face bother you?" he asked. "If it does, I can substitute a blindfold."

"No," Maggie said. "I'm okay like this. What now?"

"Patience, darling. You'll know everything in due time." As he arranged the sheet over his wife's body, Maggie suddenly realized that there were holes cut in the fabric. Herb arranged the sheet so that holes were over Maggie's breasts and her crotch. "Spread your legs," he said, and Maggie complied. Herb finished arranging the material so that her entire crotch area was accessible through the hole.

"Now for the rules." He twisted the dial on the timer. "I'm setting this for one minute. During that time, I'm allowed to touch only the parts of you that are covered by the sheet. The next minute, I'm allowed to touch only what shows through the holes. We'll play as many rounds as we want. Questions?"

The game sounded decadent and erotic. "None," Maggie said as she heard the timer begin ticking. Maggie's breathing quickened. Her husband had wonderful hands and knew exactly how she liked to be touched.

Maggie felt Herb begin at her feet and stroke slowly up her legs. The sensation of his hands rubbing her body through the cloth was exquisite, so different from the feel of his hands on her bare skin. When Herb reached her upper thighs, he switched to her arms. As he stroked and kneaded his way up her arms, Maggie heard the timer ding.

"I'm resetting the timer for another minute. During that time, I can touch only what is exposed through the holes. But, for now, I won't use my hands."

Maggie felt Herb sit on the side of the bed next to her. As she heard the tick of the timer begin again, she felt the feathery touch of the frond on her breasts.

"I'm able to watch only three parts of your body, dear, and it's amazing how erotic it is to concentrate on the pucker of your nipples as I stroke them."

As Herb flicked the frond back and forth across her nipples, Maggie felt her body tighten. Her breasts felt supersensitive because of the light pressure of the soft cloth everywhere else on her body. The frond caressed her nipples, back and forth. Because she didn't want to get too excited too soon, Maggie tried to ignore the tightening in her lower belly.

Ding.

She felt Herb's weight shift from the edge of the bed as he reset the timer. There was absolute silence as Maggie wondered what Herb had in store. Then she felt her husband at the head of the bed. He rubbed his fingertips over Maggie's face, touching her eyelids, lips, and ears through the sheet. "I can't see you, but I'll bet you're smiling," Herb said.

"Mmmm," Maggie purred. "I love it when you touch me." She felt him massage her scalp, then put his finger in her ear and mouth. She bit down gently on his probing finger.

Ding.

She heard the now-familiar sound of the timer being reset, then the sound of the ice tinkling in Herb's glass. They had used different sensations frequently during their lovemaking, so she had a good idea what was coming. She tensed her body for the familiar feeling. As she had known he would, Herb smoothed a cube across her left nipple.

"Yow, that's cold," she said.

Herb asked, "Want me to warm you up?" He leaned down and, as he moved the ice cube to her right nipple, he took the left one in his mouth. He sucked the tight bud into his mouth as he puckered the other with the ice.

As Herb alternated between the heat of his mouth and the cold of the ice, the sensations drove Maggie crazy. "Oh God, that's making me so hungry," she groaned.

"Then we'll have to do something about that." Herb suddenly pulled the ice from Maggie's nipple and ran it over her clit, causing her body to jump. "There are only a few seconds left and I want to cool you down." He pressed the cube against the opening of her cunt and pushed it in.

Maggie felt the cold sensation almost disappear as the ice sunk deep into her cunt, past the sensitive outer surface.

Ding.

"Are you going to leave that ice inside me?" Maggie asked, breathless.

"I can't touch you there now, so I guess I'll have to." Herb lifted one of Maggie's hands and began to massage the palm. Then he wrapped his hand around the base of each finger in turn and pulled gently, allowing the finger to slide through his hand. "It's like I'm milking each finger."

Maggie was going crazy. Cold water was trickling out of her cunt as Herb's hands were pulling on her fingers. Try as she might, she couldn't keep her hips still.

"You're getting so hot, baby," Herb purred. "I love to see you so hungry and know that I can satisfy your hunger or let it grow."

Ding.

Now Herb's mouth was on her cunt, sucking the combination of the icy water and her juices. As he drew her swollen clit into his mouth, she knew she couldn't hold back any longer. "Don't stop, don't stop," she cried as she climaxed. "It's so good, sooo good."

As she calmed a bit, she heard the rustle of Herb stripping off his clothes. She felt her husband stretch his body the length of hers, which was still covered with the sheet. As his cock probed between her legs, he rubbed his upper body over hers. The contrast between the feeling of his belly against hers through the sheet and his rough, hairy chest against her naked nipples was fantastic.

He entered her, and the feeling of his hot cock filling her was enough to trigger another orgasm. "Hold still and feel me come again," she screamed. Herb held his cock motionless and felt the waves of muscular contractions on his erection.

"Oh my God," Herb said. "I've never felt anything like that." He sighed, then began to move inside of Maggie's now-still body. "Yes, baby. Lie still while I fuck you." He thrust in and out, sliding through his wife's juices. "Lie so still while . . . I . . . fuck . . . you . . . good." He felt his climax flow from his body.

"Oh, baby. Your cunt is so nice." Herb's orgasm seemed to last forever, but eventually he felt his body relax. He rolled from his wife, pulled the sheet aside, and cuddled Maggie close.

Later, when their breathing had almost returned to

normal, Maggie said, "That was quite a game. Save that sheet for your next round. But I need to make one for you. I think two holes will be just right."

"Two?"

"Yeah. I think one for your cock and one for your mouth. I have some terrific ideas for that particular arrangement."

Changing your appearance can help you become a new person, one with habits and techniques different from who you are the rest of the time. But is someone new necessarily better at lovemaking? Of course not. But although different isn't necessarily better, for those who slip into a sexual rut occasionally, newness can be particularly exciting. Read this story and think about the fantasy that you can play out, beginning with a game of dress up.

LET'S PLAY DRESS UP

It must have been the saki. Looking back on the evening when their sex lives became dramatically charged, Ron and Sandy decided that it had been the saki.

The previous Christmas, Sandy had gotten a stir-fry cookbook for her husband, Ron, a gourmet cook. In the four years they had been married, they had established a Sunday pattern; Ron would prepare an elaborate new recipe while Sandy did the laundry, scrubbed the bathroom, and did a few other onerous chores.

That fateful weekend, Ron had decided to try a Chinese stir-fry shrimp dish that had required hours of chopping and precooking. The liquor store didn't stock any Chinese wine, so he had settled on a bottle of their Japanese favorite, saki. Ron was at his best that Sunday. He perfectly prepared a meal of homemade hot and sour soup, baby and mother shrimp, two kinds of mushrooms braised together, and emerald fried rice. Throughout the meal, they drank the saki, which they kept heated in a pan of warm water. Since they didn't own the traditional tiny saki cups, they used regular wineglasses. By the end of the meal, they had consumed most of the bottle.

Sandy took one look at the kitchen after dinner and winced. "My Lord," she said, "you've used every pot, pan, and dish in the house." The arrangement was that when Ron cooked, Sandy did the dishes.

"Actually, that's the second or third use of everything. I washed up as I went along, until the cooking got too overwhelming. Sorry, darling."

Sandy sighed, then giggled. "It's okay. I'll get started and see you . . . next Thursday, by the look of all this."

"I'll give you a hand," Ron said, starting to stack the pots in the wok.

"Nope," Sandy said. "A deal's a deal. You cook; I clean up." At that moment, the phone rang and Sandy lifted the receiver. After a moment's shocked silence, she shrieked, "Tommy, where are you?" Her brother Tommy had been traveling in the Far East for the past few months and had had very few opportunities to get to a phone. "It's my brother," she said to Ron as she pulled the phone into the dining area and flopped into a chair.

"Oh, Tommy, it's so good to hear from you. Tell me about your trip. I want to hear everything."

By the end of the twenty-minute call, Sandy had heard all about Singapore and Hong Kong and had finished another glass of saki. "Call again as soon as you can, darling," she said. She saw Ron stick his head out of the kitchen and wave in the direction of the phone. "We miss you, Tommy, and Ron sends his love. Good-bye."

Sandy walked back into the kitchen, hung up the phone, and looked around. The kitchen was spotless. "Wow," Sandy said. "Was I on the phone that long?"

"It wasn't as bad as it looked. I stuffed the dishwasher, did the pots, and cleaned the counters. All done."

"Thanks, baby, that's great." They spent the next half hour sharing the details of Tommy's trip.

"You know," Ron said, "you got off real easy with those dishes."

"I know," Sandy said, "and I'm sorry. I'll make it up to you."

"You sure will. It'll cost you big."

"Cost me how?"

"Well"—Ron stared at his wife's body—"I think I should get to name my payment. I want to play a game."

Sandy raised a quizzical eyebrow. "Yessss?" Sandy and Ron's games had been tailored to their sexual preferences over their four years of marriage. "Which game?"

"Let's play . . ." Ron deliberately dragged out the moment. He knew which game he wanted, but he loved the drama in making the announcement and seeing his wife's reaction. "I want to play Valerie."

When they had begun playing pretend games, it had been embarrassing to discuss a scenario that turned one or the other of them on, so they would start a game by assuming different personas. The games soon became known by the name of one or the other of the characters.

In the game that Ron had selected, Sandy would become Valerie, a hooker, and Ron would be Jean-Claude, her customer. They would pretend to meet in the living room, Jean-Claude would give Valerie some money, and then they would go into the bedroom and make love. It made everything seem illicit and daring and the game made the sex more creative.

Although the situations they set up were unusual, the activities during the game had always been rather tame— until that evening. Sandy looked at Ron. "I'm a bit blitzed from the saki and I guess that's why I have the courage to suggest a change in the game. I don't think Valerie would wear clothes like these," she said, looking down at her jeans and T-shirt. "Sit here"—she pointed to the sofa— "and give me fifteen minutes. Think about Jean-Claude and how he'd really behave."

While Ron waited in the living room, looking forward to whatever Sandy created, Sandy went into the bedroom and considered how to become Valerie. She pulled off all her clothes, then burrowed into the back of her closet. She quickly found what she was looking for, an outfit she hadn't worn since the day she'd impulsively bought it at a tag sale.

As she looked at the overly tight black-and-gold Lurex top and matching tight black skirt, she realized that somewhere in the back of her mind she had been planning a dress-up evening for quite a while. All it took was one extra glass of wine for her to suggest it. Now all she had to do was not lose her nerve. *I really want to do this,* she told herself as she pulled on black stockings and hooked them to a black lace garter belt Ron had gotten her as a gag gift.

Without additional underwear and without thinking about her heavy thighs and not-so-flat stomach, Sandy pulled on the black-and-gold outfit and a pair of gold spike heels. She felt scandalously wonderful. In the bathroom, she put on long rhinestone earrings, twice her usual eye makeup, and bright red lipstick. She fluffed out her short auburn hair, turned, and looked at herself in the full-length mirror.

"Oh my God," she said, amazed at the change in her appearance. "I *am* Valerie." She took a deep breath. "And Valerie wouldn't hesitate to entertain a customer—so here goes nothing."

Hands shaking in nervous anticipation, Valerie opened the bedroom door and walked toward the living room. As she stepped into her husband's line of sight, she extended her right hand and said, "Ah, you must be Jean-Claude. Marguerite regrets that she has no time for you this evening. I'm Valerie. I hope I'll do as a substitute."

"Holy shit," Ron said, unable to take his eyes off his wife so erotically gift-wrapped. "I mean, yes, you'll do nicely." He picked up a thick stack of phony bills they had bought at a toy store for their game.

"Just a moment, sir," Valerie said. "We need to agree on a price. I'm not necessarily going to settle for what you might pay Marguerite. What does she charge?"

Getting into the situation, Jean-Claude said, "I usually give her fifty for the evening." He peeled five phony tens from the wad.

Valerie chuckled deep in her throat. "Outrageous. For

fifty dollars, you get a look at parts of my body, nothing more." She snatched the bills from his hand. "Sit down."

Amazed, Ron sat down on the sofa. This wasn't his wife, his wonderful but slightly prim wife. This was another person entirely, and she was getting him amazingly aroused.

"Now, for fifty dollars," Valerie said, her voice husky and thick, "you get to look at my legs." She put one spike-heeled shoe up on the coffee table and used both hands to stroke her calf. "You get to see my black stockings, all the way to the top." She ran her hands up her leg, sliding the short skirt up. When she reached the top of her stockings, she said again, "All the way to the top—" she revealed one lacy black garter and about an inch of flesh, then quickly pulled her skirt back down—"but no more."

Ron's breathing had quickened. "No more than that, Valerie?"

Valerie gave a short, sexy laugh. "Well, I guess you could see one of these." She reached up and pulled the stretchy scoop-necked top down over one bare breast. "I guess you should see what you'd be getting if you bought the rest of me." She slid her hand over her full breast, then pinched her exposed nipple. "See how hard it gets?"

Jean-Claude pulled five more bills from the wad in his hand. "What do I get for this?" he asked.

Sandy slipped the top back up, took the bills from him, and slowly raised her skirt. "You get to see where I keep my money," she purred. She pulled her skirt up gradually, finally revealing her black lace garter belt and the curling auburn hair revealed by her lack of underpants. "I tuck my money in my belt here," she said, "so that no one can find it." Deliberately, she ran her fingers through her pubic hair, fluffing and preening, then folded the bills over the top of her garter belt. Then she lowered her skirt, the bills creating a bulge under the tight stretchy fabric.

She patted the money bulge, then looked at the bills still in her husband's hand.

"Since I see you can afford it," Valerie said, "for another fifty, you can see all of me."

Without hesitation, Jean-Claude handed Valerie five more bills. "Now don't move from your seat," she said.

"I couldn't move if I tried," Jean-Claude said.

"That's good. First," Valerie said, "you'll want to see the breasts. Of course, you've already seen one, but this way's so much better." She pulled her shirt off over her head. Momentarily, she wondered what had come over her, but she quickly decided that she didn't care. She liked what was happening. She looked at her husband's face, which was mesmerized by her performance.

Ron carefully shifted and readjusted his pants to allow for his increasing erection. He didn't want her to see any movement. He had never seen his wife like this and he didn't want to break the spell.

"Your breasts are very lovely," he whispered. "Can you make the nipples hard?" Now where had that come from? he wondered. Ron had been afraid of spooking his wife, but obviously Jean-Claude wasn't afraid of spooking Valerie.

She winked at him. "Usually, I charge extra, but for you, it's free." She swirled her hands over her soft breasts and pinched and pulled at her nipples until they stood out from her soft white flesh. "Like that?"

"I want to suck them," Jean-Claude said. "How much?"

She named her price and he quickly handed Valerie more bills.

Valerie leaned down and placed both hands on the coffee table. Slowly, she bent her body toward her customer. She rocked her shoulders left and right so her large breasts swayed in front of his face. Jean-Claude moved to the edge of his seat and touched Valerie's right breast. "No hands," she said. "You paid for mouth only."

Jean-Claude slipped to his knees and, trapped between the couch and the coffee table, he lifted his chin and opened his mouth. Inch by inch, Valerie moved her erect nipple closer to his lips. When it touched them, Ron sucked it into his mouth, suckling and nipping at the tender bud. "Now the other," he insisted. "I paid for both."

With a smile, Valerie swayed and let him suck on her other nipple. Then she stood back up, leaving Jean-Claude on his knees. "I forgot to put my money away," she said, raising her skirt.

"Take it off," Jean-Claude said hoarsely as she slid her skirt past the top of the garter belt. "Please." He handed her more money.

Valerie obliged by pulling the skirt off over her head and dropping it on the floor. As she noticed Jean-Claude again adjusting his clothing, she said, "Are you getting uncomfortable in those clothes? Why don't you undress?"

Ron stood up and quickly stripped off his clothes. As he reached for his wife, now clothed only in her garter belt, stockings, heels, and long earrings, she laughed. "You haven't paid for me yet. Sit back down on the sofa."

Jean-Claude, naked, with a huge erect penis poking

straight out in front of him, sat back down on the sofa. Valerie walked forward and stood between his knees. "Do you want me?"

Jean-Claude handed Valerie the rest of the money and reached for her. "Not so fast," she said. She was anxious to feel her husband's cock inside of her, but she wanted to stay in control of what was happening. "We're gong to do this my way." She raised her knee and placed it beside him on the sofa. When he grabbed for her, she slapped his hand away. Slowly, she lifted the other knee, placed it on his other side and, straddling him, lowered her wet cunt onto his hard cock.

"Is that what you wanted, sir?" Valerie asked.

"Oh yes," Jean-Claude said.

Valerie raised up and again pressed down onto his cock. "And that?"

Jean-Claude grabbed Valerie's hips, pulled her up, then slammed her down again onto his cock. Valerie grabbed his shoulders and together they established a rhythm. "Baby, baby, baby," he yelled as first Jean-Claude and then Valerie climaxed.

"Wow," Ron said, later. "That was amazing. You were amazing."

Sandy was suddenly mortified. What had she done? She thought about the past hour. "Oh my Lord." She pressed her flaming face into Ron's shoulder.

"No, baby. Don't let Valerie slip away," Ron said, understanding Sandy's mood. "She's sensational and she and Jean-Claude made wonderful love together. Please don't be upset in any way."

"Are you sure? Now that I think about the way I behaved . . ."

"Of course I'm sure."

"It must have been all that saki." Her lower lip was quivering. "I always was a cheap drunk."

"You were terrific and sex has never been any better between us. Think of it this way. Would Valerie be ashamed? Would she blame it on the alcohol?"

Sandy picked her head up and looked at her husband. "No, I don't think she would." Slowly, Sandy smiled and nodded. "I think she'd be proud of all the money she earned." She reached down, picked up the stack of bills on the coffee table and combined them with the bills from the top of her garter belt, and counted. "Wow. Valerie earned over three hundred dollars. She must be pretty good at making love."

"She is, my love, she most certainly is."

This next story demonstrates that you don't have to have intercourse to obtain sexual pleasure. I considered calling this story "Let's Play Telephone," but as I reread it, I changed the title to . . .

LET'S PLAY DOUBLE SOLITAIRE

"Darleen, honey," Karl said, "any idea when you're coming home?"

"In another week or so, I hope." Two weeks earlier, Karl's wife, Darleen, had rushed to her sister's home in a distant city soon after Alice's twins were born. "I can't leave poor Alice," Darleen said. "Toby's going through the terrible twos and the twins never seem to be asleep at the same time.

"Jason went back to work today," she continued. "I'm not sure whether he went back to the store because he was needed there or because he couldn't stand it here another minute. Toby is jealous of the babies, so he's begun wetting his pants again and he throws temper tantrums to get attention. We're trying to ignore him, but it's hard. It's bedlam most of the time."

Darleen sighed. "Oh, honey, I can't wait to get home and hug you. By the way, you'll be happy to hear that I've finally convinced Alice to hire a part-time housekeeper, at least for the first month or so. With some luck, she'll find someone soon and I can come home before we forget what sex is all about."

Karl really liked Darleen's sister, but right now, he wanted his wife back home. "I miss you," Karl said.

Darleen stretched out on the bed in her sister's guest room. It had been a long evening and was now after eleven. "I miss you, too." Darleen paused. "I can't get over how quiet it is here now with everyone sleeping." For the first time since Alice had come home, Alice, Jason, Toby, and the twins were all asleep at the same time.

"Will the quiet last?"

"Jason has agreed to help Alice with the babies tonight so I can get a full night's sleep, my first since I've been here. I'm exhausted and I'm sore all over from lifting my nephew a thousand times a day."

Karl thought a moment, then said, "I've got a good idea. Get a big towel and spread it on your bed. And get some baby oil from your makeup case. Then take off all your clothes and stretch out. I'll give you a long-distance massage."

"A massage sounds decadent and wonderful. But long distance?"

"Trust me. I've got it all figured out. Put the phone down and do it." While Darleen got the towel and the baby oil, Karl stripped down to his shorts. What he had in mind wasn't just an ordinary massage.

"Okay, I've got the stuff," Darleen said, dropping the towel on the bed. "Now, give me a moment to undress." Again she put the phone down, and Karl could hear the rustling of her clothing. "Done," Darleen said. "I'm naked as the day I was born. Now what?"

"Spread the towel on the bed so we don't get oil on the blanket and sit down. We'll start on your legs."

A moment later, she said, "Ready."

"Pour some oil in your palm and rub your hands to- gether to warm it. Then spread it on your right leg and massage it into your calf."

Darleen rubbed her oily hands over her calf, kneading her sore muscles. "Ummm, that feels great. Let me do the other one."

"You shouldn't get ahead of me, honey, but go ahead." While Darleen rubbed her other leg, Karl poured some baby oil into his palm from the bottle Dar- leen kept next to their bed. "I'm giving myself a mas- sage at the same time you are," he said. "And it feels wonderful."

Several minutes passed while the only sounds traveling through the phone lines were purrs and sighs as Darleen and Karl rubbed in the baby oil. "I need some more oil,"

Karl said, "and it's time to move on. Let's massage your arms. Pour some more oil in your hand and rub your right arm. Then move on to your left."

"This phone call is going to cost a fortune, dear," Darleen said.

"Who cares. We haven't spent anything on movies or restaurants for the last few weeks, so let's spend some on creature comforts of another variety."

Darleen rubbed oil on her arms and onto her shoulders. "God this feels good," she murmured.

"It sure does. This was a wonderful idea." He paused, then said, "I'm taking more oil and rubbing my chest now. You should, too."

"On my chest?"

"Sure, why not?"

A little shy, Darleen said, "On my breasts?"

"Wouldn't that feel good?"

Darleen shrugged. "It might at that. I just don't want to get all excited without you here to . . . you know."

"Just trust me to do what's good for you. Now rub some oil on your breasts. And don't forget your nipples." As Karl rubbed oil on his chest, he pictured Darleen stroking oil on her skin. "How does that feel?"

"Nice."

"Just nice? I think it feels sexy and erotic. I think you want to rub your nipples just a little harder. Why don't you pinch them and see how that feels."

"Karl, cut that out. You're going to make me all horny. And you're there and I'm here."

"And we're going to enjoy ourselves. Now, pinch your nipples and make them all hard and pointy." He paused, then asked, "Are you doing it?"

"Yes," she whispered. "But it feels so naughty."

"It's supposed to feel good. And naughty feels delicious, if you do it right. Look at your body carefully. Are both nipples hard?"

Darleen looked at her body, shiny from the oil. Her nipples stood out from her small flat breasts. "Yes."

"Good. Now lie back on the towel, take some more oil, and rub your belly. Make slow, smooth strokes. Put your finger into your belly button and rub it around." He heard her purr, then said, "That's a good girl. I'm doing exactly the same thing to my belly. I'm rubbing oil all over."

Darleen could hear that his voice was becoming husky. "Are you getting excited?" she asked.

"Oh yes," Karl answered. "I'm lying on our bed and my cock is getting very hard. He's standing straight up, missing you. Are you lying down?"

Darleen nodded, then realized that Karl couldn't see her. It felt strange to be this intimate and not be in the same room. "Yes, I'm lying on the bed on the towel you had me get."

"Good. Without sitting up, spread some oil on your thighs and rub it around just as far as you can reach. Rub the insides of your thighs but don't touch your pussy. I want to touch my cock, but I won't." Slowly, he rubbed his own thighs, then said, "Now, stop rubbing and stroke the inside of one thigh with your fingertips, very lightly, just barely touching your skin, then the other. I'll do the same."

She did as he asked. "Oh, honey, you're making me so horny."

"And we're not done yet. Take the towel and dry your

hands well. Baby oil isn't good for your pussy and that's where you're going to stroke next."

Darleen thought that what her husband was suggesting was indecent, but she was beyond caring. She had masturbated before they were married, but now, since she had Karl, she seldom touched herself. Karl often rubbed her clit while they made love, but they had never done anything like this. She rubbed her hands on the towel. "My hands are dry."

"Touch your pussy. Is it wet?"

Darleen reached down and touched her lips. "Oh yes. I'm dripping."

"Wet your fingers with your juice and rub them around. Explore each fold and rub your own wetness into every crevice. While you do that, I'll be rubbing oil all over my hard cock and balls."

Darleen stroked herself, mindlessly enjoying the feel of her fingers on her body. "Oh, darling, this feels so good."

"I know. It feels good for me, too. I'm rubbing my hand up and down my cock. Close your eyes and picture what I must look like while I look at you in my mind. Rub your pussy. Stroke your clit and make it feel good. Rub yourself until you lose control and come. And tell me when you're going to climax."

Darleen rubbed and caressed herself, finding the spots that gave her the most pleasure. "Good," she gasped. "So good."

Karl listened to the sounds of Darleen's pleasure while he wrapped his oily hand around his cock. He used his palm and fingers to rub the entire length of his erection. "I'm reaching down now," he said, "and stroking my balls.

It's hard not to make myself come, but I want to wait and do it with you."

Darleen could feel her own orgasm building. "You won't have to wait long," she said, her breath coming in short pants. "I can feel myself getting closer and closer."

"Don't stop rubbing. Does your clit feel all big and hard? Do you need to touch it, to rub it just right? Stroke yourself good, honey."

Darleen knew she couldn't wait much longer. "I'm coming," she said, trying to control her urge to yell. "I'm coming right now! Come with me."

Karl heard his wife's plea and squeezed his hand around his cock. He pumped a few more strokes and felt his entire body tighten. Semen squirted into the air and spilled onto his thigh. "Yes, honey," he yelled. "Oh yes."

"So good," Darleen said as she felt the last waves of her orgasm. "So good." She took a deep, shuddering breath.

"Yes, very good," Karl said, his voice barely above a whisper.

"Did you come, too?" Darleen asked.

Karl laughed. "You've got to be kidding. Here I lie in a pool of goo and you ask whether I came. Of course I did, and it was great."

Darleen nodded. "It truly was. I've never done anything like that before, but it really was marvelous."

"Don't get the idea that this replaces real sex, mind you," Karl said. "I still want you home as soon as you can."

"Of course, honey. But you must admit that what we just did will make this separation a bit easier to bear."

"Just a bit, honey. Just a bit."

* * *

This last story is an introduction to controlling fantasies, which I'll explore in more detail in the next chapter. First, let's see what happens when Bill reveals his deepest dreams to his wife. Pay particular attention to the "hand-clasping" that Suzy used to help Bill "talk about" the sexual activity he wanted most. This technique can help you communicate with a particularly reticent partner. Suzy also reassures her husband at every step that the things he's been dreaming about are okay, that he's not a bad person for wanting something out of the ordinary.

LET'S PLAY DOCTOR

Bill had always had a fantasy. Beginning when he was barely in his teens, he had dreamed about playing doctor. Not playing doctor, exactly, but playing patient and having his body examined in many delightfully inventive ways. In his fantasies, the doctor was a beautifully built woman with a large bustline and long fingers. It's funny, he thought, until recently she hadn't had a face. Now, in that favorite fantasy, honed after many years of dreaming, the doctor had a face, his wife's.

Suzy and Bill had been married for three years and their sex life was full and fun. They made love at all hours, in many places and in many ways. They had realized several of his fantasies and a few of hers. Never, however, had he mentioned his recurrent dream.

Bill's job as a salesman required a great deal of travel and, as usual, he had been away the entire past week. As often happened when Bill returned after a long absence, he and Suzy had made love almost nonstop all day Saturday. Early Sunday morning, they were lying side by side in bed, satiated from a particularly spirited romp around the bedroom, again playing out a fantasy, this one Suzy's. Lazily, Suzy asked, "We've played out so many of my dreams, I've been wondering, do you have any fantasies that we haven't played out yet?"

Slightly embarrassed, Bill answered her question with one of his own. "Why do you ask? Isn't our sex life exciting enough?" He laughed and hugged her closer.

"That's not it at all," she said. "I just love acting out scenes." She enumerated some of the games they had played. "I like master and slave, and desert island. I like pretend games. I was just hoping there were more different games we could play, that's all."

"Oh."

She sensed something below the surface of Bill's reticence. "Well, are there any more?"

"Not really."

"Bill, baby," she wheedled, "tell me."

"It's very hard to talk about such things," Bill said.

"I know. Give me a hint."

Bill was now thoroughly embarrassed. He had no idea why the idea of telling Suzy about his doctor fantasy and its peculiar wrinkles filled him with such dread, but he was sure this dream was so dirty that she wouldn't understand. On the other hand, part of him wanted her to know, wanted to act out this scenario together.

Suzy knew she was on the track of a fantasy that could

give them both pleasure. But, she wondered, what if his reluctance meant he wanted something so bizarre that she would be horrified? And if so, could she react in a way that wouldn't spoil things? But she felt the rewards far outweighed the risks.

"I know there's something you want to tell me," she said. "I understand that you're worried. Maybe the fantasy that you have will be something that will turn me off. But it won't make me love you any less or think any less of you. And I hope that whatever it is will be something that we can share and enjoy together."

Bill wanted to tell her. And he wanted to discuss the details of his fantasy, the exciting things that the doctor did to him in his dream. But how?

"Let's try something," Suzy said. "Hold my hand." Bill reached out and grasped Suzy's hand. "Now," she continued, "I'll make some suggestions. When I'm getting closer, just give my hand a little squeeze. The closer I get, the tighter the squeeze. How's that?"

Bill was silently holding her hand. Maybe she wouldn't guess. But maybe she would.

Suzy felt Bill's palm get sweaty. Whatever this was, it was something that her husband wanted to share but was afraid to. She just hoped she could be worthy of his trust. "You want to pretend to rape me."

Bill laughed at the idea, so unlike any of his fantasies, in which he was the victim, not the aggressor. "Not likely," he said. "I only play nonviolent games."

Suzy thought that if she stayed with the slightly outrageous, she might make whatever secret Bill was keeping seem tame by comparison. "You want to tie me to the bed and beat me with a seven-foot bullwhip."

Bill continued to laugh, his hand slack in hers. "Okay, you want me to whip *you*." She felt him tense. "Pain?"

"Not a chance," Bill said.

"You want me to be in control somehow." He gave her hand a little squeeze. "Wow, you mean I get to ravish your body?" Suzy said, trying to send accepting vibrations.

Bill pulled his hand away. "This is silly."

Suzy took his hand again. "No, it's not silly. It's sexy. I never dreamed you wanted anything like that. But there's a lot more, isn't there?"

Bill was silent.

"Let's see," she continued, still trying to exaggerate so his fantasy would seem tame. "You want to be my slave." No squeeze. "You want to be hypnotized and obey my every whim." Still nothing. "You want me to poke and prod every part of your helpless body." Suzy felt Bill's body go rigid. "You want to play doctor, with me the doctor and you the patient."

Bill trembled all over.

"Oh, honey," Suzy said, quickly reassuring her husband. "That sounds so yummy. I get to play doctor and examine every inch of you."

Bill was silent.

"Is there more?" Suzy asked. Bill squeezed her hand. Suzy racked her brain. What more could there be? What was it that was so unusual that it made Bill reluctant to share? Then she had an idea. "You want me to give you a rectal exam."

Bill pulled away and swung his legs around so he was sitting on the edge of the bed. "I have to take a shower," he said.

Suzy kissed the middle of Bill's back. "I understand," she said. And she did.

It was a week later. Suzy had done a bit of preparation for a fantasy evening. All the time she was hunting for and buying the few small things she would need, she found her excitement mounting. This was going to be terrific.

The following Saturday when Bill came home, Suzy was ready. After a leisurely dinner, Bill settled down to watch a basketball game and Suzy disappeared into the bedroom. He knew that they would be making love all evening, but he was waiting now, extending his enjoyment. A half an hour later, Bill heard his wife call, "Bill. Come watch the game in here, will you?"

"Sure, babe," Bill said. He switched off the TV and all the lights and wandered into the bedroom. What he saw there made his cock get hard and his knees shake. Suzy was dressed in a white T-shirt and white pants. She had a stethoscope around her neck and a clipboard in her hand. The bed was covered with a plastic sheet, which, in turn, was covered with a new crisp white percale one.

"We're ready for you now," Suzy said, her voice official and businesslike. She had had a hard time not giggling, but one look at Bill's face and she had sobered. He was in a world all his own, and obviously loving it.

Suzy handed Bill a doctor's office paper smock she had "borrowed" from her local internist. "Kindly remove your clothes, put on this drape, opening in the front, and stretch out on the table."

It was his fantasy come to life. Could he deal with it? In a daze, Bill took the smock from his doctor and turned his back. He wanted this so much. Without a word, he quickly stripped off all his clothes and put on the smock. He clutched it around his middle and slowly sat down on the edge of the bed.

"That's fine," Suzy said. "On your back, please."

Bill just did as he was told. He surrendered himself to the fantasy, and to his wife/doctor. "Now," Suzy said, looking down at her clipboard. "This is an exam for sexual reactivity." She was afraid she would freeze at the last minute, so she had made up all the details and written them down. "When was your last ejaculation?"

"You're kidding?" This wasn't going exactly the way his dream progressed.

"Sir, this is a very professional exam." Her voice hadn't lost its businesslike tone. "I repeat, when was your last ejaculation?"

Bill decided to go along with the fantasy. He answered, "Last weekend."

"Were you having intercourse or masturbating at the time?"

Bill was totally embarrassed, but he also realized that the embarrassment was extremely exciting. "I was making love to my wife."

"Do you mean to tell me that you haven't had an ejaculation since last Sunday?" Theatrically, Suzy pulled on a pair of surgical gloves, snapping each finger. She reached down, opening the smock, and fondled Bill's testicles and squeezed his erect penis. "I find that hard to believe. It's been six days. I'll bet you jerked off sometime while you were away from home. Admit it."

Bill swallowed. He couldn't believe what his wife was doing to his mind. It was hard to lie to his doctor. "Well . . .

Last Wednesday, I had a hot conversation with my wife on the phone and I got so excited . . ."

Suzy remembered the incredibly sexy conversation they had had from his hotel room. She had actually masturbated after she hung up; she realized now that Bill had also. She also knew that he was as excited by their dirty talk as she was. She filed that information away for future use.

Still sounding professional, she asked, "Exactly what did you do, sir?"

Bill couldn't imagine that he was talking like this, but he was deep into the fantasy and he had to answer the doctor's questions. "I stood in the shower, turned on the water, and squeezed some shampoo into my hand. Then I wrapped my hand around my cock and squeezed and rubbed until I came."

"I'll write that down," Suzy said, scribbling on her clipboard. "Are you very excited now?"

"That's none—"

"Sir, no need to be shy. This is a doctor's office, and I can see that your cock is very hard. Are you very excited?"

This was his wife he was talking to, but somehow it wasn't. "Yes," he admitted. "I want to make love to you right now."

When he started to sit up, Suzy pushed him back down onto the bed. "Well, the exam isn't over yet. Turn over."

He suddenly realized that she had remembered about the rest of his fantasy and she wasn't going to stop with just this part of the exam. Oh God, Bill thought. What have I gotten myself into? Be careful what you wish for, he reminded himself. You might get it.

He turned over.

Bill could hear Suzy moving around behind him. "I need to check your temperature, sir," she said. Bill felt his wife part his buttocks with her gloved fingers. Suddenly, a thin shaft of something cold and slippery penetrated his ass. "Oh God," he moaned. The feeling was spectacular. The fantasy was playing out very differently from the one in his dreams, but it was just as potent. His cock was so hard, it hurt.

While the rectal thermometer remained inside of him, he could hear his wife writing on her clipboard.

"I've made a note that your cock reacted very strongly to that anal penetration," she said. "We'll have to check those responses further." Bill felt her withdraw the thermometer. He took a deep breath and sighed. That had been very exciting, he thought. Now he was so hungry that he didn't think he could wait any longer.

"Turn on your side, facing away from me," she said. With a jolt, he realized that she still wasn't done. He needed to make love to his wife so badly, he wanted tó scream, but he also wanted to play out the rest of his fantasy. Aroused and a bit nervous about where this was leading, he did as he was told. Suddenly, he felt something cold and slippery circling his anus.

"Just some lubrication for the rectal exam." Bill's body went rigid and he felt Suzy's gloved finger slide slowly deep into his ass. He thought he would climax right then from the pure pleasure.

"Yes," she said, "your cock does react to rectal stimulation. Very good. Now we have the means to examine your responses." Suzy reached around and grasped Bill's cock with her other lubricated and gloved hand. "Now, if I ma-

nipulate your cock, I think we can observe your ejaculation."

Bill's mind whirled. Maybe he should do something,
protest, get up. But he couldn't move. It was too good.
He looked down and watched as Suzy's hand pumped his
cock. He felt her finger examining his ass, moving, probing, rubbing. He couldn't hold it any longer. As he
watched, he climaxed, spurting semen far across the
exam table.

"That was very good," Suzy said when the semen
stopped flowing. "Now we have learned what makes you
come." She bent down and kissed Bill's neck and shoulder. In a softer voice, she added, "And had a lot of fun
doing it. I love you, you know."

"Oh God, that was so exciting. I don't remember ever
being so high."

"Yes, I gathered that." Suzy stripped off her rubber
gloves and her clothes and lay down against her husband's back, spoon-fashion. She pulled up the quilt and
covered them both.

"But what about you?" he said.

When he started to turn, she said, "Don't do anything,
honey. Let's just take a little nap, then see what happens
when we wake up."

"It's really okay, what we just did?"

"It's not only okay, it was wonderful."

"But you didn't come."

Suzy hugged her husband. "You know, it's funny about
that. I got so much enjoyment from that fantasy and
watching your pleasure that it was almost as good as my
own climax." She kissed his neck. "I've thought a lot
about playing doctor since last weekend, so later, if we're

in the mood, there's a slightly different version of that fantasy that might be fun."

"Whatever you say, Doc." Then Bill and Suzy fell asleep.

3

LET'S PLAY CONTROL GAMES

Have you ever fantasized about having your wife completely under your control? She'd do anything you wanted her to do, anything. Or have you thought about being completely in your wife's power? She'd make you do wonderfully naughty things that you wouldn't dare to do on your own. And you wouldn't bear any responsibility for pleasing her. You'd only follow orders.

That's control, taken and given. Having control means that you can have your partner do whatever you want. You can take pleasure in whatever way pleases you and, by doing so, give your partner pleasure at the same time. Giving up control means you can learn exactly what gives your partner pleasure while bearing none of the burden of trying to figure out what to do and when. You can both give and receive sexual enjoyment until the line between giving and getting blurs and finally disappears.

Giving or taking control, however, isn't for everyone. It

frightens many people. It turns others off. Some have been taught that fantasies such as the ones that follow are evil and unnatural. As with so many other preconceived notions, however, these deserve to be swept aside. Fantasies about power are normal and more common than you probably would believe. So, if you find yourself getting excited by the thought of living out a control fantasy, don't censure yourself, just read on.

If, however, you're completely turned off by the idea of giving or taking control, flip to the next chapter. But if you do, you may be missing an excitingly different way to give and get pleasure.

It is important to note here that not everyone who has a control fantasy wants to live it out. Many people merely want to think about giving or taking control. Therefore, you may be able to scratch this itch by just reading to yourself or out loud as a prelude to lovemaking.

If, however, you want to learn ways to communicate this desire to your partner, use the techniques I've suggested for nonverbal communication. You might be surprised by your partner's receptiveness. Once you have begun to explore these fantasies, if you both agree, you can experiment with control games to your heart's content.

A few caveats.

First, control games are *never* to be used to force anyone to do something. At the moment that an activity becomes unpleasant for either party, it should be stopped immediately. If you haven't already done so, take a moment now to read the Author's Note at the beginning of this book. If you're not sure that both you and your partner are consenting adults, don't play control games.

They're not for you. For the rest of you, *anything done between two consenting adults is fine.*

Second, either partner has the responsibility to say no. Notice I didn't say the right to say no; I said the responsibility. If an activity is suggested and you don't think you would enjoy it, you owe it to your partner to reject the idea. And your partner must, I repeat *must,* accept that judgment.

Third, there must be a way to communicate the fact that an activity that seemed like a good idea when you began has ceased being enjoyable. I recently read the draft of a book about lifestyles in the S/M community and found that they use a very sensible two-level code-word system.

Red means stop, *now.* I don't want to do whatever we're doing anymore. If you decide to try a control fantasy, you must be able to use this word and obey it. If you can't, then don't play. Period.

Yellow means something is bothering me, but I don't want to stop altogether. Ask me what's wrong. I might want to say, "I'm cold. Turn the heat up," or "This strap around my wrist is cutting off the circulation." The two of you can fix the situation, then continue to play.

Why do you need code words? As you'll see in the following stories, in a control situation, it can be fun to yell, "Oh, stop. Oh, please stop," or "Don't make me do that. Please don't," and have your partner understand that it's all part of the fun. It's for effect. But, if you're yelling no but mean yes, how, then, do you convey the fact "I *really* don't want to do that." Use the code words.

Now you're ready to use the stories that follow as guidelines for activities you can try and ways you can successfully communicate both the positive and the negative.

LET'S PLAY DON'T LET GO

Ben and Cassie had bought the old farm knowing that it would be years before they could move in. But they loved the old house and spent almost every weekend working on it. Their first task was to clean one bedroom and fix it up with sleeping bags, a Coleman lantern, and places to store old weekend clothes.

Once that was done, they decided to tackle the kitchen. They started one Saturday morning by scrubbing the floor and counters and washing the windows. Then Cassie began working on the sink while Ben attacked the hot-water heater. "I don't think this sink is worth saving," Cassie said after an hour of scrubbing. "I can't get any of these stains out of the bottom. Especially here under the faucet."

"Use a little elbow grease," Ben said, pulling his arm out from under the heater. "There are lots more things around this place that need fixing. A new sink will have to wait."

After an hour of hard work, the stains in the old sink still hadn't faded. Although Cassie knew it was silly, the new sink had taken on a larger significance. She wasn't going to live in a slum. They could afford it, if she could just convince Ben that it was important.

COME PLAY WITH ME

Later that evening, by the light of the lantern in the bedroom, Ben and Cassie were playing their nightly game of gin rummy. Over the months they had been playing, the scores had been pretty even. "Tonight," Cassie suggested, "let's play for a prize. Whoever has the most points after, say, two hours, gets something."

"Like what?" Ben asked.

"Like if I win, I get a new kitchen sink."

"Cassie," Ben said, "there are so many things that have to come first."

"I know, but you're always up for a wager. And I really want that new sink."

"Okay," Ben said thoughtfully, "but you will have to make the other side of the wager worthwhile."

"All right. Anything you want."

"Anything . . ."

"I don't intend to lose," Cassie said. "I want that sink too badly."

"Okay. Let me get this straight. If you win, you get the new sink. If I win, I get a forfeit."

Cassie detected a gleam in Ben's eye. "What kind of forfeit?"

"I'll decide when I win." Ben's mind was already filling with possibilities.

"Well . . ." Cassie said, suddenly unsure. There was something very sensual in the way Ben was looking at her. When it came to sex, Ben had always had a very fertile imagination and Cassie always enjoyed what he thought up, but his ideas frequently took some getting used to.

"You said that you didn't intend to lose," Ben reminded her. "Chickening out? I assure you that if you do lose, you'll enjoy your forfeit."

Cassie smiled. "Okay. You're on."

Ten minutes before the end of the two-hour time period, Cassie was leading by a considerable margin. In the last hand, however, Ben was dealt four fours, a run in clubs, and two jacks. It took only three draws until he declared, "Gin" in a loud voice.

"You can't have gin," Cassie said. "I have a fortune in my hand."

Ben leered and pointedly looked at his watch. "Too bad, darling." He counted her points and wrote down the score. Even before he added the final total, Cassie knew she had lost.

"What's my forfeit?" she asked.

"Tomorrow morning."

"What about it?"

"I'll tell you about your forfeit tomorrow morning. For now, I want to consider my options."

Cassie laughed. "You're teasing me."

"Darn right. Now, beddy-bye time."

The following morning, Cassie awoke sexually aroused. All night she had had dreams about what Ben might have in mind for the morning. Some of the things she thought about made her excited, but others made her a little uneasy.

Ben, sensing her mood, hugged her naked body and said, "Good morning, love. Don't get too hung up about this forfeit thing. I promise I won't do anything you won't enjoy. And if anything makes you the least bit uncomfortable, just say, 'Ben, end this forfeit.' If you say those words, I promise I will stop right then and there. Okay?"

Cassie smiled. Why was she wary? Ben was always kind and considerate. "Sorry. I guess I got a bit carried away."

"Not at all." He reached down and slid his fingers through her pubic hair. "You're excited and very wet." He stroked her, then removed his hand. "I hope you'll forgive me, but I don't want to make love now. Just be patient and let's have breakfast."

An hour later, fed and dressed in work clothes, Cassie was ready for whatever Ben had planned.

Ben looked at his wife. She was wearing an old polo shirt but no bra, a pair of old, paint-smeared sweatpants, tennis shoes, and socks. Yes, he thought, her outfit would do nicely. "Come on outside," he said.

As Ben walked out the front door of the cabin, he was struck anew by the wonderful view. The cabin overlooked a remote mountain lake and was surrounded by lush trees and bushes. With the mountain laurel in full bloom and birds singing, the setting was idyllic. Since the house was about a mile from the road, there was no sound of traffic. There was no one around for miles.

Ben led Cassie to a maple tree with several thick, low-hanging branches. Ben pointed to a branch about head-high. "Hold on to that branch," he said, "and don't let go."

As she grasped the branch, she said, "I don't get it. You just want me to hold on here?"

Ben spread her hands far apart so if she turned her head or leaned forward, she could rest her forehead against the limb. "Yup, that's all. But just remember that this position is the result of a wager and you don't want to get the reputation as a welsher. And, as you know, reputation is everything. Of course, if we ever do this again, and if you win, you don't want me to welsh. Right?"

"Right. So I won't let go. For how long?"

"Until I say you can. Do we have a deal?"

Cassie stood up straight and saluted with her head. "Yes, boss. I won't let go until you tell me to."

"I like it that you know I'm the boss. You can call me that until the end of the forfeit."

Cassie grinned. "Right, boss."

Ben got an old blanket from the trunk of his car and folded it into a pad. "Okay, now lift your foot." Carefully, Ben removed first one tennis shoe and sock, then the other. "This ground right here is stony and I wouldn't want you to hurt your feet," he said as he placed her feet on the blanket. "This should make things nice and soft."

"It does. Now what?" Cassie was puzzled. So far this was not proceeding as she had thought it would. She hadn't known exactly what to expect, but she had been anticipating some kinky sex thing.

"No more questions. Just go along and you'll know what's happening as it happens."

Cassie sighed. Just relax, she told herself, and roll with it. Enjoy the soft breeze and the view of the sun on the lake and let whatever is going to happen happen.

Ben left her there and disappeared into the house. He reemerged a few moments later with a large pair of scissors. "I assume that you can spare these work clothes." As Cassie started to answer, Ben added, "Anyway, you really have no choice unless you want to end the forfeit."

"Whatever you say, boss," Cassie said, still puzzled.

Ben snapped the blades of the scissors together beside Cassie's ear, then started at the bottom of one leg of the sweatpants. Slowly, he cut up the outside of the pants, watching the material part. When he had cut up to the waistband, he left the elastic and her underpants intact for a moment. "How does the fresh air feel on your skin?" he asked.

"Nice," Cassie answered, wiggling her hips.

Ben leaned down and pulled the gray fabric aside. He slowly ran his tongue up the back of Cassie's knee, enjoying the feel of her shiver. As she moved, Ben said, "Just a reminder. Don't release your hands."

Cassie nodded and tried to relax. The air felt like a soothing caress on her skin. A shaft of sunlight shone across her calf and left a warm trail on her skin. Never before had she been so conscious of the feel of the outdoors.

Ben shifted around to the other leg and cut the material from ankle to waist there, too. Now the pants were only two pieces of gray material that hung between her legs, held up by the elastic waistband. "Very nice," he said as he licked the back of her other knee. "Very nice indeed." He gathered the fabric and dusted the ends along Cassie's legs. Then he cut the waistband and put the pants to one side. Now, Cassie was standing, gripping the branch with both hands, dressed in only her panties and polo shirt. Ben walked around her, appraising her looks and nodding.

"Now for your shirt." He snapped the scissors. "I'm not going to cut the whole thing off just yet. Just a couple of holes." Ben grasped the front of the shirt and, with a few snips, cut two holes in the front of it, exposing Cassie's small breasts. With the first touch of the fresh air, her nipples contracted into tiny points.

"That feels so sexy," Cassie said. "The breeze makes me so hungry. Kiss me, Ben."

"Not so fast," Ben said. "We've got a long way to go yet."

"Oh, hon."

"It's my show, darling, unless you want to call the whole thing off."

Cassie shook her head. Ben was right, it was his show, and she was going to enjoy it that way.

Again, Ben disappeared into the house and returned with a kitchen chair. "Spread your legs wide apart," he said, placing the chair facing her, close to her legs. She did so, and Ben sat in the chair, his knees between Cassie's legs. His mouth was just below breast level.

"Now, lean toward me and put your tit near my mouth. I want to suck you."

Cassie was both shocked and excited by Ben's crude language. Without letting go of the branch, Cassie leaned forward so Ben could suck on her nipple. He kept his hands folded in his lap while he drew his wife's breast into his mouth and nipped at the puckered tip. "Oh, please stop," Cassie said, knowing he would not. "You're making me crazy."

"I don't care what you want. You can beg forever, but we're going to do it my way, nice and slow." He blew a thin stream of air onto Cassie's wet nipple.

Cassie let her head fall back, relishing the exotic feelings that her husband was creating. "Now the other," she heard him say. She moved so her other breast was in his mouth. He suckled until she thought she would collapse from the pleasure. "I don't know if I can continue to stand up," Cassie said. "And my arms are beginning to fall asleep."

Suddenly concerned, Ben said, "Do you want to stop? I really don't want to make you uncomfortable."

"I'm okay for a little while. What you're doing just makes my knees weak."

"Well, then, we'll have to do something about that." He disappeared into the house again and returned with something hidden behind his back. "I've decided to let you loose, in a way." He pulled a small saw from behind his back and began to saw through the branch that Cassie was holding. "Don't let go," he reminded her. Soon, the small branch snapped and Cassie lowered her arms. Ben massaged her upper arms and shoulders while she continued to hold on to the branch.

"Now," Ben said, bending down and picking up the blanket, "follow me. And watch your footing. I don't want you to hurt yourself." He held the branch between Cassie's hands and led her to a sunny spot in the middle of the back lawn. He spread the blanket and said, "Now, lie down."

Cassie stretched out on the blanket, still holding the piece of wood. "Keep your hands at the ends of the branch and stretched over your head. I love what that position does to your body." Cassie languidly stretched her spread arms high above her head and off the end of the blanket. "Oh yes," Ben murmured. "Just like that."

"Yes, boss," Cassie said. "Whatever you want."

Ben went back to the tree and returned with the scissors. "Now for a few more alterations." He cut off the bottom of Cassie's polo shirt until it ended just at the level of her nipples. "Ummm. Sexy as hell." Then he carefully cut across the crotch of her panties. "You're so wet, darling," he said. He ran his finger between her legs. "I bet you want my penis right about now."

"Oh yes, Ben, I want you so much."

"You're always so impatient. One of the things about my forfeit is that I can teach you patience." He tickled the entrance to her vagina with his index finger, then slid it inside. As her hips began to move, he said, "So impatient. Just relax. I don't want you to come yet. And don't let go of your branch." As her hips quieted, he slid his finger out, then in again. "Don't come, whatever you do," Ben said loudly.

Cassie sighed and tried not to think about the excitement building inside of her, then said, "Yes, boss."

Ben began to finger-fuck his wife, moving his finger in and out of her wet cunt. Soon, he added a second finger, then a third. "You're close, aren't you? You're going to come even though I told you not to move."

"I can't help it," Cassie cried. "It's so good."

Ben used the index finger of his other hand to softly rub Cassie's clit. It was too much. She screamed and climaxed. Ben's cock was hard and insistent, but he wanted one more thing. He'd always wanted his wife to let him put his cock into her mouth, but she always said no and he didn't want to insist on something she found unpleasant. Now, maybe he could ask once more. He waited until Cassie had calmed.

"Darling," he said, pulling off his sweatpants. "I want to put my cock in your mouth."

"I really don't want you to," Cassie said. Even though something inside her felt that she owed him for all the pleasure he had given her, the idea of his large cock in her mouth was repugnant.

"Can you tell me what is such a turnoff?"

Cassie hesitated. It was so hard to talk about this type of thing. "I'm just afraid."

"Of what?" Ben asked softly.

"Of that big thing in my throat. And . . ." She sighed and Ben waited. "It'll taste awful and I'll disappoint you by gagging or throwing up."

"Oh, baby," Ben said. "You wouldn't disappoint me if you'd just try." He thought a moment. "I've got an idea."

Ben disappeared into the house and returned with a jar of honey. "Trust me. I'll stop anytime you want me to," he said. "You don't have to touch me, just hold on to that branch and relax."

Cassie closed her eyes and nodded. She did trust him. He would stop if she wanted.

Ben knelt beside Cassie's head, dipped his fingers into the honey jar, and spread a big dollop on the head of his erect cock. "I know how much you love this stuff. Just relax and taste." He touched the tip of his sticky erection to his wife's lips. "Just taste me."

Slowly, Cassie extended her tongue and touched it to the tip of Ben's cock. "Sweet," she said. She licked at the honey. Ben dipped another fingerful, drizzled some on his cock, and rubbed some on Cassie's lips with both his finger and his penis. With her eyes closed, Cassie found that she couldn't tell which was Ben's cock and which was his finger.

He poked his sticky finger into Cassie's mouth and she sucked the honey off. Ben hesitated, then pushed just the tip of his honey-covered cock into Cassie's mouth. As she sucked, she relaxed. She knew that Ben had the head of his penis in her mouth, but she found that it wasn't so terrible. Actually, it wasn't bad at all.

Ben smeared more honey on the shaft of his cock and pushed it deeper into his wife's mouth. He could feel his orgasm building and he knew that Cassie could feel him growing in her mouth. He couldn't risk coming in her mouth, as much as he wanted to.

Quickly, he pulled out of her mouth, moved between his wife's spread legs, and rammed his cock into her pussy, still soaked with her own orgasmic juices. It was only a few strokes before he came.

"Oh God," he said a few minutes later. "That was so wonderful."

"It was, wasn't it?" She paused, then added, "And you know, it wasn't as bad as I expected. You actually felt nice in my mouth. And it's wonderful that I can give you so much pleasure."

"You have no idea how much pleasure," Ben purred.

"Oh, I have some idea. You made me come, even when you told me not to."

Ben and Cassie giggled. "I did, didn't I?" Ben said.

This story is for anyone who's ever had a control fantasy that centered around rape. It is very important for you to realize that you're not alone. Let's define the type of rape we're talking about here. Fantasy rape is not the abhorrent violent criminal act that we read about all too often in our morning newspapers. Those crimes *are* abhorrent.

Fantasy rape is a benign, comfortable, forced sexual encounter where the hero vanquishes the heroine and makes exciting, powerful love to her. This type of rape is not an uncommon fantasy. In fact, an entire genre of women's romantic fiction, the so-called bodice rippers, revolves around this fantasy.

It is important to note that a rape fantasy is really either the desire to be dominated, to give up control of the sexual situation, or the desire to take control, to call the shots without the worry about the specifics of your partner's pleasure. In reality, the one dominated has the ultimate control because he or she is the one who says, "Stop." Thus, the one in control can do whatever he or she likes, trusting the submissive partner to call a halt if things get uncomfortable.

If you're intrigued, read this story about people like you who want to play rape. If you might be interested in playing this scene out, slip in a bookmark before you think better of it and share your desires with your partner.

Nan and TJ discovered that their fantasies were more similar than they might have imagined, and they enjoyed an evening of hot sex because of it. But every control fantasy must have limits. If you consider acting this fantasy out, pay close attention to the rules Nan sets out.

LET'S PLAY TO TELL
THE TRUTH

"I don't know how you can watch so many of those things," TJ said to his wife. "One talk show is like the other. Everyone and his brother airs his dirty laundry in public. Everything from 'I had an affair with my daughter's husband' to 'My lesbian lover's mother's best friend's wife makes me horny.' How many different ways can they tell you how to improve your sex life?"

TJ and his wife, Nan, had spent all day Saturday working around the house and, in the background, Nan had played four of the talk shows she had taped during the week. Now they sat in the living room drinking a glass of wine before dinner. "I enjoy them," Nan responded. "I like to know that there are people in the world who have serious or weird problems, ones that I don't have to worry about."

"And sex?" TJ said. "Do you have unfulfilled longings in your sex life? Do you have sexual fantasies like the people on that program said?"

"Yeah, I guess. Not 'unfulfilled longings,' as you put it, just dreams and stories I tell myself during a bad day at work or in the middle of the night. Like doing it with one of the stars of my soaps, or in a hot tub on the back porch of our million-dollar house. Don't you?"

"No," TJ answered too quickly, turning away.

"You're full of it," Nan said. "I can tell by the sound of your voice."

"I don't have unfulfilled longings, if that's what you mean."

TJ was talking too fast and his voice was pitched a bit too high. Nan was sure that he was hiding something. Softly, she said, "I think you have at least one fantasy that you won't admit to."

"Like that last program," TJ continued. "That so-called expert said that many women have rape fantasies. That's nonsense."

"No," Nan said softly, "it isn't."

TJ's head jerked around and he stared at his wife. "You're kidding. You mean you have had rape fantasies?"

"Not all the time," she said. "But sometimes it's nice to imagine being ravished by a handsome guy"—she smiled and patted TJ's cheek—"like you, darling."

TJ was silent. "To tell you the truth," he said with a sigh, "I guess I've had an occasional rape fantasy, too."

"Like what?" Nan was fascinated. If TJ also had a rape fantasy . . .

"It's not violent. It's just power, I guess." TJ leaned his head against the back of the sofa. "Mostly, I dream about sneaking into some woman's bedroom and, you know, having my way with her."

"Does she fight you?" Nan asked.

"Yes, but I overpower her. God this is hard to talk about. I feel like a pervert. I don't really want to rape anyone, you understand."

"Of course not," Nan said quickly. "And I don't actually want to be raped."

"What? Are you serious? Do you want to be raped?"

Nan nodded. "Not assault. Not painful. Just fighting someone and knowing I'll lose. And knowing that my handsome rapist will force me to service him. No choices. No decisions."

This was a revelation to TJ. Ever since he could remember, he had fantasized about rape. And ever since that first thought, he had suppressed the fantasy, thinking that he was really weird. Now his wife was telling him that not only was he all right but that she had the same fantasy.

Nan decided to break the lengthening silence. "Would you like to act it out? With me? I'd love to fight with you and know that you'll vanquish me."

TJ just stared. Trembling, he admitted, "I would like that, too."

"Wow." Nan took TJ's hand and squeezed. "But we need a few rules. I've watched enough of these talk shows to understand that there are limits to any fantasy. First, we need *out* words."

"What are *out* words?"

"Well, we need a way for me to say stop, without actually using the word *stop*. If we play this right, I want to be able to yell for help without you getting confused as to whether I really mean it."

"That sounds sensible." TJ couldn't believe that he and his wife were actually talking about acting out a rape fantasy.

"It is. On one program, some members of the S/M community talked about the words *red* and *yellow*." Nan explained the symbolism of the two words.

"Okay. That seems reasonable," TJ agreed, his excitement mounting.

"They talked about trust. You know, how I have to be able to trust that you will stop when I say so." TJ started to interrupt, but Nan didn't let him. "I have no doubts about you, darling," she said. "And I have no doubts about my ability to use the words if I need to."

TJ was confused. "I would hope that if I hurt you or anything, you'd stop me."

"There are some women who don't understand that they can say no. I can, and will, if I need to. You just have to understand and not get your feelings hurt."

TJ just grunted. He was still adjusting to the situation. He and his wife were sitting on the sofa having a discussion about his deepest sexual secret. And she wasn't horrified. She wanted to play with him. "I must be the luckiest man in the world," he said, wrapping his arm around Nan's shoulder. "You're terrific."

"You are, too." Nan rested her head on TJ's shoulder.

They sat for a few minutes savoring the building sexual tension, neither knowing how to put their ideas into motion. Finally, Nan broke the silence again. "How about if I go to bed, like in my fantasy. Then you can break into the bedroom, through the door, of course, and . . ."

"You're really feeling tired, aren't you?" TJ said, setting the scene in motion.

"I am. Even though it's only five o'clock, I'm going to sack out." Without another word, Nan started toward the bedroom. "By the way, I just wanted you to know that I'm going to be wearing an old nightgown that I was about to throw out, anyway. If anything was to happen to it, it wouldn't be a tragedy."

TJ nodded as Nan smiled and walked down the hall. Not knowing exactly what to do now, TJ sat on the sofa and thought about his fantasy. Could he get into this without all his hang-ups? He wasn't sure, but he wanted to try. He saw the light go out in the bedroom. Slowly, he stood up and, before he could chicken out, walked down the hall and into the semidarkened room.

Enough of the late-afternoon twilight showed through the closed blinds for TJ to be able to see his wife's shape under the mound of covers. He tiptoed toward the bed, planned his move, and suddenly dropped onto the edge of the bed, reaching down and covering Nan's mouth with his palm. "Don't scream," he growled, "and you won't get hurt."

As he saw the mock terror on his wife's face, he almost pulled back. But he reminded himself that it was only a fantasy. He could never do anything that would cause real fright, but her good acting was affecting him. As if she sensed his feelings, she winked. It was okay.

He lifted his hand from her mouth and used both hands to press her shoulders against the mattress.

"Don't hurt me," she whimpered. "What do you want? My jewelry is on the dresser. I don't have much money, but anything I have is yours."

"I don't want money, lady," TJ snapped. "I want you."

Nan struggled and freed herself from TJ's hands. She scrambled across the bed, but before she could get off the other side, TJ grabbed her ankle and pulled her back. "It will be easier for you if you don't fight me," he said.

Slipping out of character for a moment, Nan smiled and said, "But not as much fun." She slipped back into her role and said, "Just don't hurt me."

TJ tried to stretch Nan out on the bed, but the minute his hands released her, she tried to escape. He grabbed her wrists in one of his large hands and pulled her arms

up over her head. "Don't run away," he said in a menac-
ing voice. "What I'm going to do will be real good."

He bent over and tried to press his lips against hers.
She twisted her face away so that TJ had to use his free
hand to cup her chin and hold her face still. "I told you
not to fight me," he said. He slid his hand into the back
of her hair and held her head steady as he pressed his
mouth against hers.

Nan kept her lips pressed tightly together, fighting off
the intruder despite the fact that she knew it was her husband. She was really feeling like she was being forced to
do something against her will and it was enormously exciting. I knew this would be thrilling, she thought, but I
didn't expect anything like this.

TJ pulled back. "Open your mouth, bitch." Where had
that language come from? he wondered. He never used
words like that in real life. But here, it seemed so appropriate. He kissed Nan again. This time, she parted her
lips slightly. "That's a good girl," he said when he pulled
away. "Now, let's see what I've got here."

While one hand still held Nan's hands over her head,
TJ used the other to grasp the front of her nightgown. It
took three yanks before the garment's straps gave way
and he bared Nan's breasts. "Nice tits," he growled. He
bent down and bit one soft mound. He licked and suckled as he felt Nan squirm against him.

"Yellow," she said.

TJ froze. "What's wrong? I'm sorry." He didn't know
what he was sorry for, but . . .

"Don't be sorry. It's just that my right arm is falling
asleep," Nan said.

TJ sat up and released Nan's hands. She flexed her

arms and twisted her wrists. Then she put her hands back over her head, this time with her elbows bent. "Like this," she said.

He again grasped her wrists. "You okay this way? Are you sure?"

"Don't hurt me," she whimpered, getting back into character.

God, this is sensational, TJ thought. He bent over, continuing to nuzzle first one breast, then the other. "You've got nice tits, lady," he said. "But let's see the rest of you." With some difficulty, he pulled the remains of Nan's nightgown off without letting go of her wrists. "Yeah," he said, his eyes roaming her naked skin, "and the rest of your body's nice, too." He ran his fingers roughly through her pubic hair. "Nice pussy."

Nan was shocked and titillated by her husband's coarse language. Usually, the harshest word he used was an occasional *shit*. But the words he was using now fit the situation, and she could feel her body reacting. But she was going to fight him, and lose. She twisted, trying to get free of the hand that imprisoned her wrists.

Now, TJ had a logistical problem. He couldn't let go of his wife's wrists, but he couldn't remove his clothing with one hand, either. In my fantasy, he thought, our clothes just disappear when I want them to. Then he had an idea, if Nan would just go along. "Listen, lady, I've got this fifty-pound sack of . . ." He hesitated. ". . . something, and I'm going to put it on your hands so you can't get away. Understand?" He put the feather pillow over her hands.

She understood TJ's problem and marveled at his ingenious solution. She struggled, pretending to try to free

her hands from the tremendous weight. "Oh mister," she
said, "don't hurt me. Please let me go."

TJ smiled at his wife's cooperation, then changed the
smile into a deliberate leer. "Not a chance." He quickly
removed his clothes. "Now you'll get what you deserve."

"Deserve?" Nan said. "I never did anything to you."

"I've been watching you," TJ said, his hands roaming
over his wife's body. "You wear those tight tops so your
tits show through. And your long legs in those shorts."
His wife never wore clothes like the ones he was describ-
ing, but he found he enjoyed picturing Nan like that. "In
one pair of shorts, I could actually see the crack in your
beautiful ass. And your pussy hair, too."

"I never . . ."

"And you're going to get what you've been asking
for." TJ pushed his finger into his wife's wet cunt. "So
wet," he said. "I bet you've been imagining what it
would feel like to have me stick it into you. Now spread
your legs."

Her hands still imprisoned under the heavy sack, Nan
pressed her thighs tightly together and crossed her ankles. "Get away from me, you beast." What a corny line,
she thought, but it felt right to say it—partly like a performance and partly like the fantasy she had always wanted
to act out.

TJ wanted to take the game a small step further. He
thought about their *out* words and had confidence in
Nan's ability to tell him that he'd gone too far. He
slapped Nan lightly on her squirming hip. "Don't press
your luck, lady," he said. He felt his wife's body react instantly, not with pain but with sexual excitement. He
looked at her and, with his eyes, asked her, Is this okay?

Nan made it clear that it was okay. "Please," she said, "don't hit me. I'll do what you want." She spread her legs wide apart.

"Now that's more like it," TJ said. He crawled between his wife's spread legs and took his hard cock in his hand. He slowly rubbed the head of his penis through her wet folds. "Yes. I like a cooperative woman." He pressed his cock against her opening and shoved it roughly inside.

Usually, they indulged in long foreplay, building the excitement until they actually had intercourse. But Nan was already so excited that she didn't want any more teasing. She wanted TJ to fuck her hard right then.

Unable to use her hands, she wrapped her legs around TJ's waist and pounded her hips against him. Over and over, they slammed their bodies hard against each other until they climaxed with a simultaneous shout.

As TJ collapsed on top of his wife, she pushed the pillow from her hands and hugged him. "Holy cow," she said, panting. "That was unbelievable."

"And you, darling, were amazing. You knew exactly how to play the scene. It was better than my best fantasy."

"I knew nothing. I just did what I wanted to do."

"Well, then, our fantasies are remarkably similar."

"I guess so," Nan said. "It was great."

"And the slap?"

"Nothing like that ever happened in my dream, but it felt right when you did it. Not too much of that in the future, however. I don't think I'm into pain as pleasure."

"I'd like to experiment occasionally as long as you know what to say if I go further than you like."

She nodded. "That sounds fine." Then Nan raised her

eyebrows. "You mean," she said, trying to sound amazed, "that rapist is liable to come back?"

"He might. You never know."

The final story in this chapter is about pain. In our last story, Nan told TJ that she wasn't into pain as pleasure, but some people find that a small amount of pain heightens their senses and becomes pleasurable. If you think that you or your partner might enjoy a slap or a spank, read on. If, however, you find this idea a turnoff, skip this story and turn to the next chapter.

Remember that, as I've warned before, these fantasies should be acted out *only* by those who are ready to accept the responsibilities discussed previously. Pain should *never* be used to force anyone to do anything, nor should it ever be used without the consent of both partners. Doris and Barry have been using pain as a part of their lovemaking for a long time and they have developed a fantasy world in which they both enjoy playing.

LET'S PLAY SCHOOL

"You've been doing very poorly in all your classes," Doris said to her husband.

Barry immediately picked up on his wife's cue. They had ventured into off-center sex early in their relationship and now it took few cues to begin a game. Obviously,

Doris wanted to play teacher and student, one of their favorite role-playing games.

"I'm sorry, Miss Gilbert. I'll try to do better." He smiled as he remembered the real Miss Gilbert. She had been his seventh-grade English teacher and he had fantasized about her when he was in her class. He had never dreamed that his wife would not only understand but would be an eager participant in his fantasy life.

"I don't think that's good enough," Doris said. "I may have to call your parents."

"Oh, please don't call them," Barry said. "I'll do anything."

"I don't know. I haven't made my mind up quite yet. Step into my office while I consider your punishment."

Barry lowered his head and stared at the floor. "Yes, Miss Gilbert."

Her back ramrod straight, Doris led Barry into the den. She walked around behind the large desk and sat down. Barry took his position standing in front of the desk, eyes lowered. Doris picked up a ruler and slapped her palm with it. "You've been very bad," she said. "You'll have to convince me that it won't happen again. If you can do that, I might not have to call your parents, after all."

Barry's voice trembled. "I'll do anything."

Slap. Barry watched the ruler hit Doris's palm and he felt his cock harden.

Slap. Doris enjoyed this part, making him wait. She loved building the sexual excitement she could read in her husband's eyes.

Slap. "Yes, I guess you will do anything. Assume the position," Doris said.

Barry bent at the waist and flattened the upper half of his body on the desktop.

"You're more of a fool than I thought," Doris snapped. "Leaving your pants on like that earns extra punishment. Stand up and drop your jeans before you bend over."

Barry knew exactly what was going to happen, so his hands were shaking, making it difficult to unbuckle his belt. When he finally had the belt open, he undid his jeans and let them fall around his ankles.

"Shorts, too," Doris snapped. "Drop 'em."

Feeling like the naughty schoolboy whose role he was acting out, Barry let his shorts fall around his ankles and, before Miss Gilbert could see his hard-on, stretched his upper body back over the desk. As usual, he was very aroused.

"I think ten for the schoolwork and five more for forgetting to pull down your jeans. Count them for me, out loud. Say thank you for each one. Do you understand?"

"Yes, Miss Gilbert."

Doris slapped the ruler smartly across Barry's exposed buttocks. She thought back to when they had first played this particular game. She remembered how difficult it had been for Barry to convince her that he really enjoyed being slapped like this. She still couldn't really understand it, but she accepted the fact that being swatted across his ass was an arousing experience for her husband. And it led to some of the greatest sex they had.

"One. Thank you, Miss Gilbert."

She smacked him again.

"Two. Thank you, Miss Gilbert."

She continued smacking him, mostly light slaps, with an occasional harder one thrown in.

"Eleven. Thank you, Miss Gilbert."

Recently, they had discussed this part of the fantasy and Barry had asked her to hit him harder. He had promised her that if it got too much, he would use their phrase, "Holler uncle," to tell her.

Doris brought her arm back and slapped her husband very hard. As she looked, she saw a wide red stripe appear where she had hit him.

"Twelve. Thank you, Miss Gilbert."

What she was doing was obviously all right with Barry, so she hit him again, hard.

"Thirteen. Thank you, Miss Gilbert."

Doris shook her head, not understanding but accepting. Again the ruler came down across Barry's buttocks.

"Uncle," Barry said.

"Oh, baby," Doris said, upset that she had hurt him. "I'm so sorry. I didn't mean—"

Without straightening from his bent-over position, Barry interrupted. "Don't apologize. It was exactly what I wanted. I just didn't want number fifteen to be that hard. Enough is enough." He took a deep breath. "Fourteen. Thank you, Miss Gilbert."

Doris smiled. She would never have believed that they would be communicating so openly about their desires, but it was wonderful. She tapped him on his back with the ruler.

"Fifteen. Thank you, Miss Gilbert." Barry straightened up and rubbed his backside. "Now you won't call my parents?" he asked.

"Well, you have to show me that you can be obedient," Doris said. The fantasy usually ended at this point and they went into the bedroom and made love. Today, she had decided to add a little spice to the mix. "Come over here." She knew that she could ask anything of her husband, but he wouldn't do something he didn't want to. He would merely holler uncle.

"Yes, ma'am." This is a new wrinkle, Barry thought. I wonder where it will lead. Barry hobbled around the desk, his pants and shorts still around his ankles.

"Look at your dickie," Doris said, tapping Barry's erection. "It's sticking straight out. That's lewd and dirty. You'll have to learn not to get so excited."

Barry was embarrassed. He didn't know exactly why, since he and his wife had been making love for more than ten years. Somehow, however, Miss Gilbert had never seen him this way. "I'm sorry, Miss Gilbert. I can't seem to help it."

"Well, young man, it's naughty, and I know exactly the right punishment. Kneel down."

Not knowing what to expect, Barry knelt on the rug at Doris's feet. "Take off my panties," Doris barked, lifting her full skirt.

Barry looked at his wife's undies. She was wearing tiny flowered underpants over a white lace garter belt and white stockings. He reached up and began to pull the panties down. "With your teeth, I think. Put your hands behind you and use your teeth."

With difficulty, Barry grasped the panties in his teeth and, by alternating sides, managed to get them to the floor. He knelt in front of Miss Gilbert, head down.

"That's very good, young man," Doris said. She sat in the desk chair, her legs spread wide and her skirt around her waist. "Now look at your dickie. It's still hard. I bet you want to stick it in me. Well, young man, you have another think coming. You must learn discipline." She grabbed the front of his shirt and pulled him toward the chair. "Lick," she ordered.

Momentarily, Barry was shocked. Miss Gilbert wouldn't . . . He smiled. He had gotten so far into his fantasy that he had forgotten that this was his wife. He leaned into her lap and touched her open cunt with his tongue. Slowly, he stroked her flesh with his tongue, first with the tip, then with the flat—short strokes, then long ones. He could taste her juices and it thrilled him so much that his body hurt.

He straightened up. "Was that good enough?"

"You're doing very well, you naughty boy. But I didn't tell you to stop." He kept licking, his hands still clasped behind his back. He could feel her heat and knew she was close to coming. He licked faster and faster, tickling and probing until he felt her body tense and heard her breathing quicken. He stiffened his tongue and stuck it as far into Miss Gilbert's pussy as he could.

As Doris felt her orgasm approaching, she grabbed the back of Barry's head and held it against her body. "Don't stop. Don't stop." With her husband's tongue dancing over her pussy, she came.

Barry felt her climax and sat back on his haunches. He looked down at his hard cock, bobbing and hungry. When she calmed, she said, "That was very good. Very good indeed. Now, get a warm facecloth and clean me off."

Barry grabbed his pants as he started to stand. "Leave your pants exactly where they are, around your ankles. It will help teach you humility."

"Yes, Miss Gilbert." Barry hobbled into the bathroom

and soaked a facecloth in warm water. He returned to the den and saw that his wife hadn't moved. He knelt at her feet and used the cloth to wipe gently up her juices. Then he put the cloth on the desk.

"Now, young man," Doris said, "I see your dickie is still hard. You better do something about that. While I watch, I want you to masturbate until you come."

"What?"

"You heard me. Stroke your dickie. Squeeze it and pull it until you come. I want to see it."

"But . . ."

"Are you arguing with me? Will I have to tell your parents what a naughty boy you are?"

"Oh no, Miss Gilbert. Don't tell them."

"Then do as you're told. And don't spill any of that goo on the floor. Use that cloth when you come to catch all that stuff."

Barry was humiliated but unbelievably hot. It was not his wife who was asking him to masturbate; it was his teacher. And she wanted to watch. He hesitated.

Doris picked up the ruler and slapped it into the palm of her hand. "Now, young man."

The sound of the ruler snapping into her palm was arousing him and urging him on. He wrapped his fist around his cock and rubbed. With his other hand, he reached between his legs, stroking his balls. He allowed his head to fall back and his eyes closed.

"Oh no you don't," Doris said. "Watch your hands. I want you to watch and see what I'm seeing—a naughty boy playing with himself."

He looked down and imagined how he must look. That was the last straw. Semen flowed from deep inside and he just had time to grab the cloth from the desk and catch his come as it spurted. "Oh my God," he gasped.

He cleaned himself off and, still on his knees, looked at his wife. "Oh, baby, that was wonderful."

Doris giggled. "It was, wasn't it? Was it really okay for you? I got a bit carried away."

"I could have stopped anytime I wanted," Barry answered, "but I didn't want to. Wow. What a sensational addition to the teacher and student game."

"You enjoyed it? You certainly are a naughty boy," Doris said. "It's going to take a lot of correction before you learn any manners at all."

Barry grinned and nodded. "Yes, Miss Gilbert."

4
LET'S PRETEND

Slipping out of yourself and becoming someone entirely new often opens the door to activities that are deliciously different from the ones that you usually indulge in in the bedroom. If Jane, the dutiful, hardworking wife and mother wouldn't dare to do the dance of the seven veils for a man, Jasmine, favorite of the maharaja, would. If Carol, secretary and full-time partner, wouldn't think of actively seducing her man, Gabrielle would.

In this chapter, I'll present several stories of men and women in erotic situations, which you can use in several ways.

One way to enjoy these stories is just to read one or two to get you in the mood and then make mad, passionate love to your partner. Use new ideas, positions, and locations. Another way to enjoy these stories is to read over your partner's shoulder or read one aloud. It's hard for many of us to use these explicit words and to describe vividly such erotic situations without getting very embarrassed. Try it, anyway. The embarrassment is very exciting. Try handing your partner a particularly juicy section and insist that he or she read it aloud.

The third way to enjoy these stories is actually to act them out. It's silly but very liberating. You can do things when you pretend to be another person that you might not do at any other time. And your partner will frequently find the same freedom.

How can you create a persona? Invent costumes that fit the situation, using whatever you can find in your closet. Haunt garage sales for more ideas. Use appropriate jewelry, makeup, and perfume. Put on a pirate's leather vest or a lacy courtesan's bustier. Then change your voice to fit your new image. Get into the character and act accordingly. Deviate from the story wherever you wish. Giggle if you want. But however you use these stories, read, relax, and have fun.

THE SULTAN AND THE TRADER

Once upon a time, there was a trader named Tyler. As a young man, he had gone to the Middle East from England to make his fortune. For more than ten years, he had bought and sold various precious objects throughout the desert countries. Tyler—his first name was never used—traveled back and forth throughout the Holy Land, through sheikhdom after sheikhdom, trading in spices, gold and silver objects, jewelry, and rare objects d'art. Everywhere he went, he was welcomed, everyone anxious to know what treasures he was bearing this trip. And, most important to all, he was an honest trader, always dealing fairly with both buyers and sellers.

One day, he rode into an oasis controlled by a sheikh named Murad and found the camp in turmoil. "What's happening?" Tyler asked a young boy.

The boy explained. "Cyra, the sheikh's favorite wife, is very ill. The holy men are sure she's going to die, but the sheikh still prays for a miracle. He has sat by her bedside for three days and nights, refusing food or drink. We are sad for her and we are also afraid that if she dies, the sheikh will, as well. Then what will become of us?"

"Where are they?" Tyler asked. The boy led him to Cyra's tent. After he explained who he was to the guard, Tyler was allowed to enter the tent. Inside, it was very dark, with women crying quietly. Through the gloom, Tyler could make out the form of Murad, a man with whom he had spent many pleasant hours in the past.

"Murad," Tyler said, "I am your humble servant." Murad turned, and Tyler was appalled at how drawn and gaunt the man looked. Murad turned back toward his wife.

Tyler looked down at the sick woman. "What is her illness?" he asked.

"She has a sickness of the brain," a wise man seated in the depths of the tent said. "She is raving, talking to people who aren't here, listening to voices that only she can hear."

Tyler knelt down. "May I touch your wife?" he asked

the sultan. The man nodded and Tyler felt the woman's forehead. "She's burning with the fever," he said.

"We know that," the wise man said, "but there's nothing to be done."

"That may not be entirely true," Tyler said. "I have a small quantity of bark from a special tree that a tribe in the south swears can ease the fever. They showed me how to brew a tea with the bark. I will brew some for Her Majesty, if you like."

The wise men argued that nothing could save the woman now, but the sultan knew that Tyler was an honest man, and he realized that he had little to lose. "Make some for her," the sultan said. "Please, Tyler, make her well."

Carefully, Tyler brewed the tea, using exactly the amount of bark that the tribal physician had showed him. When the tea was cool, he fed a few drops to Cyra. Over the next few hours, every time he could, Tyler fed a bit more of the cool tea to the sick woman. When she had finished the entire cup, Tyler joined the sultan, waiting for some results.

Only an hour later, Tyler heard the woman moan. He felt her forehead and it was cool. "The fever's gone, sire," Tyler said, "and she's sleeping comfortably. I think your lady will recover."

"Thank God," the sultan said. "We will celebrate tonight."

That night, a lavish feast was held in the sultan's tent. Tyler, in the place of honor, ate rare delicacies and drank fine wine until he thought his stomach would burst. There were servants to cater to his every need. After dinner, the sultan had each of his harem girls do a special dance in thanks for his wife's recovery.

When the last girl had finished her dance, the sultan said, "Tyler, they are all beautiful, are they not?"

"Oh yes, sire. They are all very beautiful. Perfect in every way."

"I thought you admired the one in the scarlet silks the most."

Tyler closed his eyes as he remembered that particular girl, a sensuous golden-skinned woman with long black hair and green eyes that seemed able to see into his very soul. "She was lovely."

"Then she's yours," the sultan said.

"What?" Tyler said, his eyes wide.

"We have made a trade. You gave me your cure for my Cyra and you will receive Zora for all the time you're here. I can not allow you to take her with you when you leave, of course, but for all your days and, most certainly all your nights, she'll be yours."

When Tyler started to protest, the sultan silenced him with a look. "It would be an insult for you to reject her. An insult to her because she will think you don't think her beautiful enough and an insult to me because you reject my offering."

Tyler looked down. "I didn't mean to insult you," he said softly. "I will, of course, be grateful for your gift."

Later, when Tyler left the feast, he discovered that the sultan had had a special tent prepared for him. As he was led inside, he could smell incense burning, but he could see very little, since the only light was one small oil lamp in the far corner. Then he saw her. Zora was still dressed in her scarlet harem dress, and the lamplight made the threads of silver twinkle. She bowed her head. "Good evening, lord," she said. "I am very honored that you chose me. I want to make your every dream come true."

"I'm a little embarrassed, Zora," Tyler said. "I didn't intend for this to happen. I don't want to take advantage of anyone, least of all you."

"Take advantage, my lord?" Zora said, puzzled.

"You know. You're here at the order of the sultan."

"I'm here because I want to be with you. I knew why we were dancing for you and I did my best to make you choose me. Every time you come to camp, I watch you, wondering what wonderful things we could do together. I never dreamed that I would be lucky enough to have all this happen." She bowed her head. "Will you allow me to serve you? Please."

Tyler leaned down and cupped Zora's chin with his hand. He raised her face so she was looking into his eyes. "Oh yes," he said, "it would be my honor and my pleasure."

Delighted and excited, Zora quickly stood up. "Let me remove your garments," she said, quickly removing Tyler's clothes. "Now, my lord, stretch out on these cushions and let me show you all the wonderful things I can do to give you pleasure."

As Zora indicated, Tyler stretched out on his stomach, trying to get comfortable as he lay on his already-huge erection.

Zora giggled. "I can see you are hungry for me, but I don't want you to be in a hurry. We have all night and I want to prolong all your pleasures." She poured a bit of fragrant oil into her palm and rubbed her hands to-

gether until the oil was hot. As she gently placed her
palms on Tyler's back, she said, "So tense. You feel so
tense. Let me rub your back for you so you can relax and
enjoy." She rubbed her hands over Tyler's shoulders,
down his upper arms, and over his back, deeply massaging his tight muscles.

"Ummm," he moaned.

"Oh yes, purr for me, my lord. Tell me you are enjoying what I do." As she spoke, she rubbed Tyler's ribs with
her fingers and his spine with her thumbs. She pressed
on various nerve endings in the way she had been taught.

Tyler was amazed at the feelings that her hands created. He was both hungry and satisfied all at once. His
body was aroused, but he felt that he could maintain that
level of excitement for hours. He could lie here forever.

Zora poured more oil into her palm and, when it was
warm, she began to rub Tyler's buttocks. Deeply, her fingers worked into his flesh, her thumbs deep in the crack
between his cheeks. Suddenly, he felt the tip of one
thumb press on his anal opening. The feeling was so intense that he was afraid he would come right then. As
quickly as the finger was there, it was gone, and his body
relaxed.

A minute later, she again touched him there and again
his body reacted swiftly. "You like that. Don't answer," she
said, "because you would deny it. It is viewed as something bad, but it isn't. It's another place that I can give
you pleasure. And, if you spill your seed now, we can take
a wonderfully long time to get you ready again."

She poured more oil on her hands and massaged
Tyler's buttocks, sliding her fingers deep between his
cheeks. When she felt him tighten, she said, "Don't fight

the feelings. Ride the crest of the wave. Go with it and take your pleasure." She pressed an oily finger against his opening and allowed it to slip inside.

As she pressed harder and the finger slid deeper into his body, Tyler could stand it no longer. "Oh God," he said. "Oh God." His muscles tensed and he came, his erect cock pressed between his belly and the satin cushion he was lying on.

"I love to watch you take pleasure," Zora said. Then she turned him over. When she saw his face, red with embarrassment, she said, "Don't be ashamed. All you did was show me in the best way that you liked what I did. That is the best compliment you could give me." She stood up and walked to a basin, which she filled with heated water. She wrung out a cloth and knelt down next to Tyler's drained body. "Let me wash you, my lord," she said.

She rubbed the cloth over Tyler's cock and balls, cleaning off the remains of his orgasm. She continued to stroke his penis with the cloth until she could feel him reacting again. "You see," she said, a smile lighting her face, "I knew you were a special man."

"And you, my dear," Tyler said, "are something special indeed."

"And we have all night to sample the many joys I know."

"All night," Tyler said.

THE SPOILED PRINCESS

Once upon a time, there was a beautiful princess named Melissa, with long raven hair, deep blue eyes, and ivory skin. She had the figure of an angel, tall and slender, with a tiny waist. But she had the heart of a brat. Because she was an only child, she had been spoiled all of her life by both her mother and her father. She had everything she wanted, and anyone who got in her way was quickly dispatched to the farthest corner of her father's kingdom. So far, she had exiled five nannies, seven tutors, three ladies' maids, and a gardener, whose only fault was to take too long to cut a perfect rose for her from the top of a bush.

Now that she was of marriageable age, her father had arranged for Melissa to marry the prince of a neighboring kingdom. The king pondered his problem: how to break the news to his daughter. He found the only possible solution. He told the queen to talk to the princess.

The queen searched out her daughter and finally found her in the garden behind the palace. "Dear," the queen said, "I have some news for you." She decided the only way to break the news was to say it straight out. "You're to be married."

"Married?" Princess Melissa shrieked. "To whom?"

"To Prince Harold," her mother said, twisting her handkerchief in her slender fingers. "Dear, I'm sure you'll be very happy. He's perfect for you. He's almost thirty, very rich, and his kingdom adjoins ours. We'll be able to visit you on occasion without having to travel too far."

"Is he handsome?" the princess asked. "I won't marry anyone who's not handsome."

"I have no idea," her mother answered honestly. "I've never seen him. But I'm sure he's very handsome. After all, he's a prince."

"If he's not the most beautiful man in the world, I'm not going to marry him and that's that."

"Why don't we wait until you meet him. I'm sure he'll be just wonderful."

"And when will we meet?" Melissa asked.

"Well . . ."

Melissa knew that something wasn't right about all this. "Well what, Mother? There's something you're not telling me."

"Now, dear, I don't want you to be upset."

"More upset than I already am, you mean. All right, Mother, tell me everything."

"He's coming here in two weeks."

Melissa knew her mother too well. "And . . ."

"F-f-for the wedding."

"The *what*?" Melissa shrieked.

"Your father and King Everett have arranged everything. You see, Prince Harold has to leave very soon for a long state visit to many other kingdoms and everyone thought it would be a good idea for you to go along. So the wedding had to be scheduled quite soon."

"Quite soon! *Two weeks*? And I haven't even *met him*."

The queen shrugged her tense shoulders. "I'm sorry, darling, but that's what was decided."

"Of course I wasn't consulted!"

"But dear," the queen said, "why should you have been?"

Melissa pouted but decided to be silent until she met Prince Harold. After all, he might be wonderful. But if he wasn't . . .

Two weeks later, on the morning of the wedding, Prince Harold finally arrived. Storms and flooded roads had kept him from arriving before the wedding as he had planned. Three hours before the scheduled ceremony, Melissa walked toward the gold salon to meet her fiancé for the first time.

As she passed various members of the prince's entourage, she noted with pleasure their looks of appreciation. She looked sensational and she knew it. She had dressed in her most becoming gown, knowing that there would be plenty of time to change into her bridal gown, if, and only if, she approved of the prince.

A footman opened the salon doors and she saw her husband-to-be for the first time. She was shocked. He was not handsome, not a bit. He was about five foot five, so he only came up to the princess's forehead. He had a large nose, soft brown cowlike eyes, and he was losing his hair. No. Absolutely not. She would not marry him.

"You're a silly little man," she said before any introductions were made. "You're not at all beautiful and I won't marry you."

Princess Melissa continued matter-of-factly, "No one can make me do anything I don't want to do." Then she turned on her heel and stormed out of the room and up the stairs to her chamber.

When the king and queen learned of their daughter's

behavior, they were appalled but not surprised. "I'm terribly sorry, Prince Harold," the queen said. "She's a bit high-strung."

"She's used to getting everything she wants," the king said.

"She's a spoiled brat," the prince said. "But we're officially betrothed and we're going to get married in a few hours, whether she wants to or not."

"Of course you're right. And someone will have to talk to her," the queen said, taking a small step backward.

"Yes, someone will certainly have to talk to her," the king said, sliding his foot behind his wife's.

"I'll talk to her," the prince said, his voice deceptively soft. "And don't worry. We'll be on time for the wedding." He took a deep breath and walked out of the salon, followed by several of his retainers.

With the help of a footman, he found the princess's chamber up the stairs at the end of the hall. "Stay out here," the prince said to his guards, "and don't open this door for anyone. Hold it shut if you must, but let no one in or"—he paused—"out."

"Yes, Your Highness."

Prince Harold opened the princess's door, walked inside, and saw the princess sitting on her divan on the far side of the room. She looked up as the prince closed the door behind him. "What are you doing here?" she asked. "I really don't want a scene. Why don't you just toddle back to your kingdom and pick on someone else."

"Because I intend to marry you," the prince said softly.

"Don't be ridiculous. I simply won't marry you."

The prince crossed the room and sat down next to his betrothed. "You *are* going to marry me. Both our families want it and both families have signed documents, pledged their loyalty, and made arrangements. We will marry."

"Let them unsign the documents and unmake the arrangements."

"Didn't any of your tutors tell you not to judge a book by its cover? I'm easy to get long with, steadfast, and well versed in subjects we can enjoy together. And I'm really a nice, peaceful man." He paused, then added, "Most of the time."

"I'm sure you are," the princess retorted, her voice condescending. "I'm sure you are. So be a nice, peaceful man and run along."

"Have you no respect for the wishes of your parents and my parents? Have you no honor?"

"Honor be damned. I won't marry you and that's all there is to it."

"You really are a brat," the prince said. "But you certainly are beautiful." The prince grabbed the princess's shoulders, pulled her toward him, and quickly planted a short but very passionate kiss on her Cupid's bow mouth. "Now be good and get ready."

The kiss was really very nice, the princess thought, but she couldn't let the prince get away with taking liberties. Without really thinking about the consequences, she thrust out her hand and slapped the prince hard across the cheek. "Get out."

His cheek smarting from Melissa's slap, the prince tightened his hold on her shoulders. "You, my love, need a good spanking, and I may do just that, regularly, after we are married," he said through gritted teeth. "But for right now, you need to learn some manners."

Not giving the princess a chance to react, the prince wrapped his arms around her and pressed his lips against hers. As he felt her squirm, he deepened the kiss, slowly dipping his tongue into her surprised mouth. It didn't surprise him that she stopped struggling as his tongue roamed the moist, hot interior of her mouth. He had had many women in his youth and he had learned from every one.

The princess was amazed at how erotic a kiss could be. She'd been kissed occasionally in the past, when a suitor got a bit carried away, but they had been light, silly pecks on the mouth. She felt this kiss from her mouth to her knees. Her skin felt hot and it was as though there were butterflies doing a dance in her lower belly. This wasn't just a kiss; it was an invasion. His tongue was taking over her body and her soul. She knew her body was no longer responding to the dictates of her mind, and, as much as she was enjoying it, she couldn't let this happen. With a last burst of control, she pulled away.

"If that's an example of the boorish behavior I can expect, it's all the more reason that I won't marry you."

The prince held her, now letting his hungry mouth roam over her neck. He nipped her earlobe and licked the hollow of her throat. "You don't really want me to stop, do you?"

"Of course I do," she said, with more conviction in her voice than in her heart.

The prince slipped one hand down the bodice of her dress and cupped her breast. Her nipple was hard and erect against his palm. "You talk a good game, my dear," he said, "but your body tells me something different." He pinched her nipple and heard her sharp intake of breath. "Yes, princess, I know."

"You do not," Melissa said, wiggling out of his grasp. "You know nothing." She tried to stand, but her trembling legs wouldn't hold her weight. With a deft movement, the prince pulled her down into his lap.

"Why don't you give up this pretense," he purred, his mouth close to her ear. "You're hot and hungry. You need my loving and secretly don't want me to stop."

"You egotistical lout," she said, her voice hoarse and her breath coming quickly.

"Let me show you." He slid his hand under her petticoats and touched the joining of her thighs through the fabric of her pantalettes. Calmly, he slid his hand up to the waist of her underdrawers, pulled at the ribbon, and slid the material down. He touched her bare flesh. "Feel how hot you are, how wet. You want me."

The princess's body went limp as the prince's fingers roamed her wet folds. "You shouldn't . . ."

"Oh yes, I should. I certainly should." He stroked the insides of her thighs. "I have a lot of experience with women, experience that won't continue after our marriage, of course." He ran his fingers up to Melissa's cunt and slid through her wetness. "I know how to give pleasure and I know when a woman is enjoying what I'm doing. You're a sensual woman, Melissa, and I know that you want me, but you're too stubborn to admit it." When she was silent, he stopped stroking her and said, "Aren't you?"

She needed for him to touch her again, but she wouldn't admit it, not to him. "I am not stubborn," she whispered, her entire body trembling. "Not at all."

He resumed rubbing her clit, which was hard and erect. "You need that. You want me to rub and touch you because it feels so good." He felt her shake her head no. "You say no, but your body betrays you, my love. I can feel how wet you are, how hungry for my loving."

Melissa squirmed. "I'm not."

"Don't try to deny anything, my dear," the prince said, slipping a finger inside the princess's body. "I feel your hunger. Your muscles want to pull me inside. You need me to rub you here." He stretched her with two of his fingers. "And here." He rubbed her slippery clit. "And if I rub you just right," he said, alternating between her pussy and her clit. "I can make you come, right here on my lap."

"You cannot," Melissa said, her voice barely audible.

"That sounds very much like a dare, but I love a challenge. I can make you come, just as I can give you pleasure all the nights of our life together." He rubbed and stroked, using all his skill to drive Melissa toward orgasm. "I can press hard," he said, pressing his finger against her clit, "or I can just tickle you." And he did.

"Nooo," she moaned, unable to control her hips, which moved now in rhythm with his fingers.

"Oh yes. I'll make you come, and then I'll spend my life giving you pleasures you've never dreamed of." He knew that she was close, so he leaned over and whispered in her ear. "Oh, I think you're ready to come." He thrust his tongue into her ear as his fingers plunged into her wet cunt. "Right now." And she did, waves of pleasure coursing over her body.

"That was so good," she purred a few minutes later. "I didn't know anyone could do that."

"Now you know. And that's just a taste of what's to come." He helped her off his lap and stood her upright. "Now, my dear," he said, "put on your wedding dress and let's get married. I'll meet you downstairs in one hour."

"Yes, my lord. Most certainly." She hesitated. "But it will take me at least two hours to get dressed."

Oh well, he thought. Marriage to Melissa would be fun, but it wouldn't be easy.

THE PRINCE AND THE CAT

Once upon a time there was an ugly cat who had wandered the countryside for many months. The cat was dark brownish gray, with a black-striped tail that had a kink about halfway down. His fur was scruffy, with missing patches and irregular spots. His eyes were mismatched, one blue and one yellow. No one in the village would feed the cat, ugly as it was, so he had to live out of the garbage. For the last week, he had lived outside the kitchen door of a huge castle, existing on any scraps he could find in the palace refuse.

One evening, after the princess and the two little princesses were finished with their dinner, Prince Albert lingered at the table, discussing royal business with his chamberlain. By the time they were done, it was well after ten and there were still a few serving platters on the gigantic dining table.

Since the prince hadn't needed the staff anymore, he

had graciously allowed all the serving helpers to leave the kitchen area. As the chamberlain left the hall, the prince realized that he didn't want the meat to spoil, so he took the leftovers to the kitchen. When he and the one remaining cook had put all but a few scraps away, the prince took the leftovers out behind the kitchen.

"Meow," the ugly cat said, smelling the delicious bits of meat and gravy in the prince's hand.

"That's a nice kitty," Prince Albert said, spying the ugly cat. He set the platter down and watched as the cat finished every scrap. "You're a very hungry kitty," the prince said. "But don't you worry. No one in my kingdom goes hungry. I'll have the staff bring you something each night."

"Brroow," the cat said, rubbing his scruffy fur on the prince's velvet pantaloons.

The prince reached down and scratched the scruffy animal behind its ears. For the next week, each evening someone would bring a plate of scraps for the cat.

Exactly a week from the night of his first feeding, the cat silently made his way into the palace and up to the prince's chamber.

"What are you doing here, kitty?" the prince said when he spotted the animal in his bedroom. He reached down and rubbed the cat's head. The cat turned over and the prince squatted down and scratched that special cat spot between his front legs. "You look a good deal healthier than when I last saw you."

"I am healthier," the cat said.

"You can talk," the startled prince said, pulling his hand back.

"I most certainly can," the cat said. "You see I'm not

really a cat at all. I'm an elf who was condemned to walk the earth as a cat for a full year. In the seven months since my enchantment, no one has been kind to me, until now."

"Well, you may live here in the palace until the end of your enchantment," the prince said. "We'll keep you warm and well fed."

"No," the cat said. "In the months since my imprisonment in cat form, I've learned a lot, and I've never gone hungry. I'll continue to wander and learn. However, since you've been so kind to me, I'll use my power to grant you one wish."

"That's very nice of you, little friend," the prince said, "but I have no need of wishes. You see, I'm a handsome prince and I'm married to a beautiful princess. I've two delightful children and all the riches I could wish for. My people love me and I love being their prince."

"Are you and your princess happy?"

"She's a wonderful, kind, and loving woman and when we met, we fell madly in love with each other. When we married eight years ago, we were told that we would live happily ever after."

"You haven't answered my question," the elf/cat said.

"Well, forever after is a long time. I love Princess Claudine very much, of course, but . . ."

"May I guess that you find yourself slightly bored in bed," the cat said with a wink.

The prince sighed loudly. "A little."

"You could use your wish to get several harem girls to make all your fantasies come true," the cat suggested.

"I don't want to be unfaithful to my wife," the prince said. "As I said, I love her very much."

"You are truly a good man. You have one wish, and that's a lot of power for the creative man. Why don't you think about it for tonight and I'll meet you here at this same time tomorrow evening. Then we can decide how to help you and your princess relieve your mutual boredom."

"You think she's bored, too?"

"I'm sure of it. Think well over the next twenty-four hours and then tell me what you wish." The cat lifted his kinked tail and proudly walked out of the chamber.

All the next day, the prince could not think about anything but the wish he would make. He considered, then discarded, many ideas. He didn't want to make the princess unhappy by requiring something she wouldn't like. But he didn't know what she wouldn't like. He found, as he thought about it, that he knew very little about what the princess liked about their sex life. Finally, he realized what he wanted.

That evening, the cat sauntered into the royal bedchamber and jumped up on the silken coverlet on the prince's bed. "Have you made a decision?" the elf/cat asked.

"I have," the prince said. "I want you to put a spell on my wife so that, for one night while we make love, she will tell me everything she likes and doesn't like."

"That's almost too easy," the cat said. "Are you sure that's what you want? I could do so many more exotic things for the two of you."

"That's what I want," Prince Albert said.

The cat flicked its crooked tail. "Consider it done. Tonight, from the moment you enter your wife's bedchamber until you leave, she will easily tell you everything you want to know."

"Oh thank you, dear cat," the prince said. "Thank you so much."

"Pooh," the cat said, wiggling its whiskers. "It was nothing. Now I will be on my way. Enjoy your evening with your wife."

As the cat neared the door, the prince said, "And if you ever need anything, don't hesitate to come back here."

"Good-bye," the elf/cat said, "and have a good night."

As the cat left the prince's room, Albert was already opening the doors to the huge wardrobe and pulling out his royal dressing gown. "This will be an evening to remember," he said to himself. "It surely will."

Only moments later, the prince walked into his wife's bedchamber. "Oh, Albert," the princess said, "I'm so glad to see you. You've been so preoccupied all day, I was afraid something was wrong."

"Nothing is wrong," the prince said. He walked over and wrapped his arms around his wife's waist. "Claudine," he said, "I love you so much." He gently kissed her cheek.

"I love it when you kiss my cheek," she said, "but I love this better." She cupped the prince's cheeks with her palms and kissed him gently on the lips. "Yes, you taste so good."

"Show me what you like when we kiss," the prince asked.

The princess ran the tip of her tongue around the edges of the prince's lips. "I like this," she said, then she nipped at his lower lip with her teeth. "And this."

The prince reached up and slid his hands around her

slender neck and into her long golden hair. His fingers rubbed her scalp until he felt her lean back against his hands. "Umm," she purred. "That feels so good."

The prince watched his wife's eyes close and he flicked his tongue over her eyelids. "Does that feel good?" he asked, knowing that she would answer truthfully.

"Oh yes," she whispered. "It feels wonderful."

The prince kissed her face, then nibbled his way over to her jaw and up behind her ear. When he nipped at her earlobe, she giggled. "I like that," she said, "but it tickles."

"Is that bad?" he asked.

"I guess not. It does feel so good."

They kissed for long minutes, the prince exploring his wife's face and the princess sliding her hands up and down her husband's back.

"Is it getting hot in here?" the princess said.

"Maybe you should get out of some of those warm clothes," the prince suggested. "Let me help you." He turned her around and began slowly unbuttoning her gown. As he undid each of the dozen tiny buttons, he kissed the area exposed. When her gown was unfastened, he lifted the heavy cloth over her head and laid it on the lounge chair. He quickly removed her several petticoats and tight waist cincher.

As the prince started to guide Claudine toward the bed, she pointed to the thick hearth rug and said, "I'd like to lie with you there, by the fire."

Dressed in her chemise, silk stockings, and slippers, the princess settled gracefully by the fire. She patted the rug beside her. "Sit here by me," she said, "and help me off with my stockings."

The prince knelt beside his wife and slipped his fingers

beneath one satin garter. "Oh yes," he said, "we have to remove this." With torturous slowness, he pulled the garter down, stroking his wife's legs through the silk of her stockings.

"The other one, too," she said as the first garter pulled free of her foot.

"Your wish, my love, is my command." In the same slow manner, the prince removed his wife's other garter. "Now your stockings."

The top of her stocking was at about midthigh. "I can't quite feel the top of the silk because your legs are so smooth and silky themselves," the prince said, making slow circles with the tips of his fingers on Claudine's inner thigh.

"Keep looking," the princess said. "I'm sure that in five or ten minutes, you'll find what you're looking for."

"Do you like it when I stroke you there?" the prince asked, taking advantage of the cat's power.

"Oh yes," she said. "I love it when you caress me."

The prince bent over and licked the inner thigh he had been stroking. "And when I do that?"

"I love that, too. Don't stop. You feel too good."

After stroking and licking for some time, the prince finally found the top of his wife's stocking and pulled it off. It took almost as long to find the top of her other stocking. "You look so beautiful in the firelight," the prince said.

"As do you, my lord." She reached up and pulled the dressing gown from her husband's broad shoulders. "You are so beautiful." She ran the palms of her hands over Albert's smooth, hairless chest. "So beautiful."

The prince relaxed under his wife's hands until he

hungered for the feel of her naked flesh against his chest. He untied the ribbons, pulled her chemise down, and, as she lay on the rug, slid his chest over her erect nipples. Back and forth, he teased her nipples with his chest and relished the feel of her skin against his. When he could take the sweet torture no longer, he buried his face in the hollow of her throat and licked her neck. He felt her pulse pound with the tip of his tongue.

"That feels so good," she said, "and makes me hungry for you." Quickly, the two lovers removed their clothes. The prince placed Claudine on her back, her legs spread so he could kneel between then. "Would you kiss me here," she said, hesitatingly indicating the hot, hungry spot between her legs. "I know that you do that sometimes, and I like it so much."

The prince was delighted. The cat's power must be tremendous, he thought. He had never known that his wife liked for him to kiss her and lick her, so the prince had ceased doing it. "Oh yes, my princess, your wish . . ." He bent over and stroked the golden hair between Claudine's thighs. "Right there?" he asked, running a finger through her juices and across the erect nub of flesh between her swollen lips.

"Yes. Stroke and kiss me right there."

The prince rubbed his finger over her, then leaned down and flicked his tongue back and forth over her hot clit. As he explored her folds with his tongue, he could hear and feel her purr. Over and over, he licked first lightly, then delved into her warm cunt. "How about this?" he asked as he sucked her clit into his mouth.

"Oh yes," she said, "just like that."

He sucked, licked, and nipped at her until he could

feel her arch her back, pressing her body more tightly against him. He took one finger and, as he drew her flesh into his mouth, inserted it deep into her body. He slowly pulled the finger out and pushed it back in. When he felt her juices flow, he added a second, then a third finger until he was sucking her clit and fucking her cunt. "Not yet," she cried. "Not yet. I want you inside me."

He pulled back and quickly pressed the tip of his hard, erect cock against her opening, then pushed, driving deep into her.

"I want you to hold your cock very still inside me," she said, "and stroke me until I come. I want you to feel my body when I climax."

He did as she asked, using all his willpower to hold still as he rubbed her clit.

"Oh yes," she said, "feel it. Share it with me. I'm going to come." He kept rubbing. *"Now,"* she screamed.

He had never felt anything like it. Her body rippled over his cock, squeezing him and pulling his orgasm from him. Sensing his need, Claudine said, "Come with me, darling."

The prince thrust over and over into his wife's sweet body. He wanted the feelings to go on and on, so, for as long as he could, the prince resisted the urge to climax. When he could hold back no longer, he grasped the princess's buttocks and slammed his body against her. "Good," he yelled as he came deep inside of his wife. "Yes, yes, yes." He collapsed on top of her and they slept.

When they awoke a bit later, they hugged each other tightly. "That was wonderful," Claudine said.

"Yes, it certainly was," the prince said.

"And to think that I doubted that cat."

"What cat?" the prince said, suddenly suspicious.

"Well, a few nights ago, I started feeding the ugliest cat you've ever seen. Out by the kitchen."

"Was he a scruffy grayish brown animal with eyes of different colors and a kink in his tail?"

"Yes, as a matter of fact, he was. Did you see him?"

"You might say. What happened when you fed him?"

"He said he was an elf and gave me one wish. I wished for the power to tell you the things I liked for us to do in bed together. I guess I wanted more than the . . ." She stammered, not wanting to admit that their sex life hadn't been perfect.

Albert grinned at his wife. "Well, I met the cat, too," he said, "and I made a wish that you would tell me what you liked in bed."

"Truly?" Claudine said.

Albert nodded his head.

Claudine laughed. "You mean we wished for the same thing and the cat had nothing to do with it."

"Who knows what power the cat had. I just know that this was the best night we've had together in a long time, and, however it happened, I'm grateful."

"Me, too. Most assuredly, me, too."

5
LET'S TELL STORIES

For this chapter, I've written several story starters, "let's pretend" stories that set up a fantasy situation similar to the ones that most of us dream about. The only difference between these stories and the ones elsewhere in this book is that these stories stop just where the story gets interesting. When the writing stops, that's where your imagination takes over.

Settle back and get comfortable with your partner. Read a story out loud and then, when I stop, you continue with dreams and fantasies you've had but have never shared—ones that I've not included so far. Flow with it. Reveal a few deliciously naughty secrets.

And if your partner is telling you a story, listen and remember. He or she is telling you something very special, a fantasy that you've been unaware of until now. Reinforce the good feelings that the sharing brings. Try to find out whether this is a fantasy to talk about or one to act out and continue accordingly. Realize that revealing your deepest dreams can lead to some of the most exciting sex you can imagine.

Many of the stories in this section depict encounters between people who begin the story as strangers. We all know by now that sex with someone whose sexual history is nonmonogamous is a high-risk activity and must never be undertaken without a condom. These stories, however, are fantasies and in them the characters behave as though they existed in a perfect, nondiseased world. In our dreams, our world can be as we wish it to be.

And remember that anything can happen in a fantasy because it happens in your mind. There are no good or bad fantasies. There are no illegal or immoral activities in fantasies.

Read, reveal, and have fun.

THE DESERT ISLAND

Monique had been on the island for more than two weeks. It was almost as though, after all the time Victor had been marooned here, the gods had finally rewarded him. He remembered the day she'd arrived so well.

"Help me," the voice had called. "Someone please help me."

Victor hadn't been sure he'd really heard anything. He had cocked his head and perked his ears.

"Help me!" There it was again. He ran down to the beach and waded into the surf. "Help me, please!"

Then he saw it. The remains of a small lifeboat on the rocks at the east end of the small bay. "Hang on," he called. "I'll help you."

He ran along the shore until he reached the rocky outcrop, crossed the slippery rocks, and waded into the breaking surf. Since he had been on the island, he had explored the rocks at both high and low tide and he knew the area well. Carefully, he made his way out through the breaking waves, stepping from boulder to boulder. Finally, he was within a few feet of the small, broken craft.

"You'll have to jump," he yelled. "Can you swim?"

"I'll have to try."

"Those heavy skirts will just weigh you down," Victor yelled.

The girl removed her brocaded dress and, wearing only her camisole and pantalettes, bravely jumped into the water. Victor moved away from the rocks, trying to guide the girl toward shallower water. "This way," he cried, pointing to a calm area beside a large rock. Then he dived into the breakers.

Together, they managed to get back to shore. Both crawled up the beach until they were away from the reach of the waves. Then the girl collapsed.

In the two weeks since that day, Victor had learned a lot about her. She was almost nineteen and had been on her way to the New World to marry a French planter. She was pretty, with golden curls that reached her waist, soft green eyes, and flawless peaches-and-cream skin that had tanned to the color of a ripe apricot.

Since she had no clothes other than her camisole and pantalettes, it was all too obvious that her body was lushly curved. It was all Victor could do to keep his hands off of her. Now he was wondering why he held back. What did the gods expect of him?

They were shipwrecked—together. And they had no idea when, or even if, anyone would find them. In the almost two years that Victor had been on the island, he had not seen a sail. When his ship went down, it had been hopelessly off course. And Monique had been drifting in the lifeboat for almost a week before she arrived at the island.

During his stay, Victor had learned to fish, found fruit and bird's eggs, and had managed to make himself almost comfortable. Now that he had the final comfort, should he choose to do something about it?

That evening, Monique and Victor sat beside the fire, as they did every evening. "What are you thinking?" Monique said after several minutes of silence.

"I'm thinking about how beautiful you are and how lonely it was here before you arrived."

"And . . . ?"

"And how much I want to make love to you," Victor admitted.

Monique sighed and smiled. "I find you very attractive, but I was afraid you didn't find me sexy. I've been waiting for you to ask or to make some move toward me." She smiled at him and raised one eyebrow. "Now that we've established what we're going to do, well, why don't you start by kissing me?"

THE COLONIES

How he had gotten here was still a foggy memory. Grant remembered being near the waterfront. He recalled the sharp pain in the back of his head, then nothing until he awoke on board a ship bound for the Australian colonies. He was a prisoner of His Majesty. One of his many enemies must have paid some brigands to shanghai him. Now he was on land again, about to be sold at auction.

The bidding was spirited. His well-developed body made him promising material, a strong laborer to work on someone's farm. When he was finally sold, he really didn't care or notice to whom. It wasn't long after that he was helping a man he assumed to be an overseer load supplies into a farm wagon.

"Just climb in and settle down in the wagon," the man said, "and don't give anyone trouble. Mind yourself and we'll all get along just fine."

Why fight? Grant thought. If I escape, I've nowhere to go. These look like decent people, so maybe this is where I make up for my carousing as a youth. Oh, well. For now I'll make do with whatever comes my way.

"What's taking you so long?" a woman's voice said. "I thought we'd be ready to roll long before this."

"Sorry, Miss," the overseer said. "I've just finished load-ing, with the help of our new man here. Name's Grant and he's ours now." He pointed toward Grant, who turned and studied the owner of the soft feminine voice.

"Mornin', Miss," Grant said, looking into a pair of the bluest eyes he'd ever seen.

"Well," the woman said, "he's certainly good-looking and well built." Her eyes roamed over Grant's body, shirtless and wet from the sweat of his recent exertion. "Very well built."

Grant looked the woman over. Well into her twenties, she had a luscious body and a more than pretty face. This might not be too bad at all. The woman walked over to Grant and ran her hand over his hairy chest and broad shoulders. "My name's Gwen and you belong to me now. You just have to keep me happy and we'll get along just fine."

"Keep you happy?"

"Oh yes, Grant. It will be your job, or I might say your assignment, to keep me happy in all ways." She tweaked one of Grant's small nipples, then ran her hand down his chest and past his belt so she could cup his balls through his pants. "In all ways, you belong to me."

Grant took a deep breath. "Yes, ma'am," he whispered. "I will endeavor to make you happy in every way."

THE OLD HOUSE

"Come on, guys, this isn't necessary."

"Listen, virgin man, you can't stay innocent all your life."

Nick tried to free his arms from the grip of his three best high school buddies as they propelled him down the darkened street. "I'm really not a virgin. I've been with girls."

"That's not what Sally says. She told Jill, who told Andrea, who told me that you didn't even know where to begin when you were up in her room last weekend."

Nick tried not to hate Sally. She had been nice to him that evening, not teasing or making fun, but she obviously did have a big mouth. So what if he'd fumbled a bit? So he'd barely gotten inside her when he's shot his load. Maybe he wasn't as experienced as these guys. So what?

"Listen," Al was saying. "We all started somewhere."

"We all started the same place." Harve giggled. "A wonderful old house right outside of town. And that's where we're taking you."

"That's right, Nick," Bud, the third of the trio, said. "Violet is the best. She's, well, she's gentle and a good teacher."

"You all learned about sex from the same person?" Nick was horrified but excited, too.

"Yup. It's sort of a tradition around here. You're new to this town, so we have to fill you in about how things are done. It's called 'visiting the old house,' and we have all done it, in our time."

"Violet does this as a favor. She enjoys introducing guys to the wonders of fucking. She's not a hooker or anything like that. She's like Mrs. Robinson in that movie."

"And is she stacked! Tits like marshmallows and a pussy that's hot and sweet. I sort of wish I was in your shoes."

Nick had relaxed a little. "Can't you see her now if you're so anxious to?"

"Nope. She's like an initiation, then it's over. She

spends one entire night with you, then it's good-bye. That's her rule."

They arrived in front of a small frame house on the outskirts of town. Bud knocked on the door and, when it opened a crack, slipped inside. Nick could hear mumbled words, then his friend came back out. "She's not busy this evening and she'd be glad to 'entertain' you."

"Come on, Nick." The three buddies propelled Nick up the porch steps toward the door. The door opened and Nick saw a woman of about forty, well built, with long, wavy hair, deep brown eyes, and a soft smile. "Good evening, Nick," Violet said sweetly. "Come in and have some coffee with me. We can talk about this and that."

"But . . ." He turned around and saw that his friends had left.

"No *buts*," she said, her voice melodious and low. "Come inside with me. You'll find I'm a patient woman with a lot to share."

Nick hesitated, then walked through the door. "Yes, ma'am," he said as the door closed behind him.

THE SECRET CLEARING

Carol had lost track of how long she'd been walking. Since she'd become separated from the rest of the group, time had lost its meaning. Why had she insisted that her father take her along on this mad junket? A lost tribe right here in the middle of Mexico. What hogwash.

She knew that when she had realized she'd gone off alone, she should have sat down and let the members of the expedition find her, but she'd become restless. And anyway, the country was so beautiful and primitive and they'd find her quickly enough. How far away could they be? Now, however, she was starting to wonder how far she'd come through this thick jungle and whether she'd be found so easily, after all.

Suddenly, she knew she was not alone. "Hello!" she called, hoping to help the searchers find her. "Hello!" There was no sound but the birds and animals resuming their movements after her loud interruption.

Carol walked a little farther and again was sure someone was watching her. "Who's there?" she called. "Come on, show yourself."

Without warning, a man appeared in front of her, standing there staring and smiling, not making any threatening moves. Not bad-looking, she thought, tall, dark, and quite handsome, if you go for the macho type. And that fantastic body with those gorgeous rippling muscles, all of which she could see, since he was wearing only a loincloth.

Her mind whirled. She wasn't afraid because the man carried no weapon and held his hands out, away from his sides. Holy cow, she thought. Maybe this is the lost tribe my father's been searching for. What a discovery. I wonder whether there are any more of them.

She heard a soft rustle and looked behind her. There was another man behind her and another to her right and one to her left. And they all looked remarkably alike, all gorgeous. They stared but made no threatening moves. Quite the opposite, she thought. They seemed intent on making her understand that they were friendly.

"Okay," she said softly. "What now?"

The four men spoke softly among themselves in a language that Carol couldn't understand. As one spoke, the others made soft humming sounds, hauntingly melodious. She hoped they would decide to take her to their village. She was tired and hungry and, in addition, she wanted to learn everything about their culture for her father. She listened intently and, although she had no idea what they were saying, she felt warm all over and strangely relaxed.

The men finished their conversation, started to walk away, and motioned for her to come with them. When she didn't immediately follow, one man smiled, pointed toward a path through the trees, then gently took her hand. Carol was surprised at how soft his skin was.

Their village was not far away. The group of women working in the center of the cluster of thatch houses looked up and smiled as she approached. A few children played in a compound behind one roughly constructed house. When they saw her, they giggled and pointed.

The men showed her to a structure off to one side of the village and motioned that she should enter. Inside, several women surrounded a large tub filled with warm scented water. "Bath," one woman said as she motioned for the others to leave.

"You speak English," Carol said, surprised.

"Words," the women said, holding up four fingers. Carol assumed she meant that she only spoke a few words. Carol wondered where she had learned them.

"Noma," the woman said, pointing to herself and grinning.

Carol smiled. "Carol," she said.

"Bath," the woman said again, and Carol willingly pulled off her boots and socks, slacks, shirt, and underwear. She climbed into the warm water and soaked her tired body.

As she looked around the bathing building, Carol saw several statues of large-breasted, naked women, each with a wreath of flowers on her head. Each woman was in the same position, seated, with hips thrust forward, knees and legs spread, hands beckoning. The figures were so blatantly erotic that Carol had to look away.

Noma appeared again next to the tub. "Eat," she said, handing Carol a piece of strange fruit. Carol took a bite and allowed the heavy, sweet juice to run down her face and into the water. While she ate a few of these unusual delicacies, Noma washed Carol's body, unbraided Carol's blond hair, and washed it with a fragrant soap. Over Carol's mild protests, Noma then dried and combed it, and, as Carol stood up, handed her a cloth to dry her body.

When Carol's body was dry, Noma handed her a soft garment of a flowing white material and motioned for her to put it on. "It's too nice," Carol said. "I can't wear this." Knowing the woman couldn't understand her words, she handed the garment back and shook her head.

Carol watched as Noma groped for a word. "Yes," Noma said, extending the garment toward the guest, then added, "Please."

Carol smiled and agreed. Noma was so open and anxious to make her happy that Carol couldn't disappoint her. She reached for her underwear, but Noma shook her head. "Please," she said again, moving Carol's underwear out of reach. So Carol put the dress on over her bare skin, enjoying the feel of the soft, delicate fabric against her naked flesh.

Noma escorted Carol from the bathing building to the center of the camp and motioned for her to sit by the fire. The members of the tribe formally greeted her in their language and gave her a bowl of delicious thick stew that tasted of hauntingly familiar but unidentifiable herbs and spices and a beverage that resembled ale.

After the meal, the women moved so that they were sitting in a large circle with Carol at the center. Then the men pulled a group of branches aside and Carol was staring at a life-sized wooden version of the statues she had seen in the bathing building. As she watched, the men moved in a circle around the statue and began to hum the same strange melody that they had hummed when they'd found her. As they passed an intricately carved bowl, they dipped their hands in a fragrant oil and began to rub the statue with their slippery palms. Carol watched as they massaged the wooden breasts and thighs.

As the men continued their erotic massage, one man, a leader, she assumed, applied fresh oil to his hands and rubbed the heavy lips between the statue's legs. Carol heard the women join in the humming and felt herself become hot all over.

Finally, after several minutes of erotic rubbing, the leader oiled his hands again, turned to Carol, and gazed into her eyes. Carol couldn't look away as he approached her, his oiled hands extended before him. Slowly, the other men oiled their hands and stood behind the leader, their hands also beckoning. She knew they wanted to touch her, to massage her as they had been rubbing the statue, but they paused, giving her the opportunity to say no if she wanted.

Then she heard Noma's voice from the women's circle. "Please," she said.

Carol, no stranger to sexual encounters, had never dreamed of anything like this. She looked at the group of men, so expectant but so controlled. She couldn't, could she? She hesitated, but neither the leader nor the men behind him made any move toward her. "Please," she heard Noma say again.

Finally, Carol made her decision. She nodded. "Yes," she said. "Yes."

THE OLD WEST

How had she gotten into this mess? Kate wondered. But she knew all too well.

It had only been two months since Sam Peck, the new foreman, had arrived. The first time she saw him, she was aware of how handsome he was, wide shoulders, narrow hips, and a lean body muscular from hard work. He wore no guns but carried instead a fierce-looking bullwhip. It was said that he had killed a man with a gun once and had not carried one since.

New foreman indeed. She had fought with him and

with her father. Why couldn't she continue to run the ranch as she had since the accident four years earlier when her father had been thrown from his horse? He hadn't been able to leave the house, so Kate had ridden the range, tending to all the details of the ranch. Now this stranger had countered most of her orders, remaking decisions that had already been made, changing procedures that had worked for many years.

The ranch was running well, Kate had to admit, but she could have handled all of it, and handled it well. And now this. It had happened by accident. They had been checking on a fence several miles from the house when the storm had hit. They had taken refuge in a line shack and the rising water had trapped them there alone, overnight, until three ranch hands had found them the next day.

Of course, Sam had been a perfect gentleman that night, but no one would believe that. If they didn't marry, she would be ruined. So, this morning, in the church she had attended since she was a child, Kate and Sam had been married and the festivities had lasted most of the day. Now, Kate sat on the sofa in the foreman's house, on the land she had loved ever since she could remember, married to a man she hardly knew.

She jumped when she heard a sound outside the door. Then Sam entered, dressed as he had been that morning, in a black jacket, plaid shirt, and denim pants. He was handsome, Kate had to admit, and he was her husband now.

"G-g-good evening, Sam," she stammered. "I wondered where you were."

"I was giving you time to get ready," Sam said, his voice soft.

"I didn't know what to do," Kate said. "I've never been married before." She realized how inane she sounded, but she was unable to stop the silly words that came from somewhere inside her. "I guess if I could remember my mother, but you see she died when I was three. She never told me . . ."

Sam walked across the large room and sat down beside her. "We're married now," he said. "Do you know what that means?" When Kate nodded, Sam continued. "Do you know what's expected from a bride on her wedding night?"

"I'm not stupid," Kate snapped. "I know what goes on." She stopped, then began to shake. "I just don't know exactly. . . ."

"It's all right," Sam said, stroking the back of her hand with a calloused finger. "It's going to be all right. It's going to be wonderful."

"It is?" Kate heard herself say, then wished she could pull the words back.

"You're so lovely," Sam said. "I guess neither of us wanted to be here just yet, but I've known about my feelings for you ever since I got here. I had a feeling that eventually we'd be married. And I'll make it good for you, you'll see."

Kate lowered her eyes and stared at the finger stroking her hand. "You will?"

"Oh yes, I certainly will."

THE DORM

She had been aware of him for a long time and had hidden pictures of him in her notebook. Recently, she had even tacked one to the wall over her bed. Brad, the captain of the college wrestling team, had his picture in the school newspaper frequently. His wrestling singlet showed off the kind of body that made all the girls drool. But Patsy knew she had no chance. Brad had all the girls he wanted.

Patsy looked at herself in the mirror on the wall of her dorm room and sighed. "You're not really bad to look at from the front," she told her reflection. She sucked in her stomach and expanded her chest. "But my boobs are too flat and my stomach isn't."

She dropped onto her bed and stared at the picture of Brad on her wall. "I'm glad that Carla moved off campus and now I can do what I want with this room." She stroked the picture, then reluctantly moved to her desk to finish her science project.

The next afternoon, she was called into the dean's office. "Patsy," Dean Howell said, "I have a favor to ask of you."

"Of course, Dean Howell," she said, happy to repay all of the help the dean had given her.

"Brad O'Hara. You must know who he is. Captain of the wrestling team."

Patsy swallowed hard and could barely get any words out. "I know who he is."

"He's flunking Geology One."

"You mean rocks-for-jocks? How could anyone . . ."

"He's a reasonable student in math and English, but the sciences baffle him. We tutored him through basic bio, but now he needs this course to stay eligible for wrestling. The state championships are coming up and . . ." He let the sentence dangle.

"You want me to help him?"

"If you would. I wanted someone with her head on straight. Brad has a talent for turning girl's heads. Then so much time is wasted. But you're so levelheaded."

Patsy smiled. If he only knew. "Of course, Dean Howell. I'll help in any way I can."

"You've got two weeks until midsemester, when he'll have to pass his exams. I'll have him get in touch with you."

That evening, Brad phoned Patsy in her dorm room. "I think I know who you are," he said. "You were in my lit class last spring."

Patsy was amazed. She would never have guessed that he knew her from Adam. "I was," she said softly. "Dean Howell spoke to me."

"Good. I need help, bad. Where are you?"

She told him her dorm and room number. "I'll be right over," she heard him say. Breathless, Patsy hurried around her room, picking her clothes up from the floor and tossing them into the bottom of her closet. She slammed the closet door and looked around. As she heard Brad knock, she spotted the picture of him on her wall. "Just a minute," she called, and ripped down the photo. Taking a deep breath, she opened the door.

"Hi," he said, offering his hand, "I'm Brad."

She shook his hand and invited him in. "The dean told

me that we have a lot of work to do," she said, trying not to stammer. "Where shall we start?"

They worked together every evening, and soon Patsy began to feel comfortable with him. Brad worked hard and studied on his own between sessions. Besides an occasional romantic thought, Patsy managed to get through the sessions and actually found herself liking her pupil as a person, not just a hunk.

The evening before Brad's midsemester exam, they worked until 2:00 A.M. "Wish me luck," Brad said as he opened the door.

"Good luck," Patsy said, bitterly disappointed that it was all ending. "Let me know how it goes," she said softly.

The next afternoon, the phone rang. "Hello," Patsy said.

"It's me," Brad said, "and I just got out of class. Professor Fairfax graded my exam right on the spot. And the answer is . . ." He paused.

Patsy giggled. "Don't tease. Tell me."

"Eighty-one. I'm eligible, and terribly grateful." She could hear him draw a deep breath. "Patsy, I'd like to come over and celebrate."

"I'd like that," she said, holding her breath.

"I'm on my way."

Five minutes later, Patsy opened the door and Brad burst in. He engulfed her in a bear hug and kissed her hard on the lips. "You're wonderful," he said. Then he kissed her again, more softly. "You really are." He cupped her face in his huge hands. "You know, it hasn't seemed right to do anything more than study, but I've been thinking a lot about you." He ran his fingers through her hair. "Your hair is just as soft as I thought it would be."

Patsy could barely talk. "Brad, what are you doing?"

"I'm doing what I've wanted to do for two weeks. And I'm going to do a lot more—that is, if you think you might enjoy it. We've been together so much, I feel we've been dating for long enough." He put her hand on the front of his sweatpants. "I want you. It feels like I have wanted you forever."

"But . . ."

Brad loosened his arms. "I'm crazy about you, but I'll leave if you don't feel the same way." He turned away.

Patsy reached up and pressed her hand against his cheek, turning his face back to her. "I'm crazy about you, too."

"Wow." He beamed. "I was so nervous and so hot. We can go to dinner if you'd like. I won't rush you."

"You rush me by merely being here," Patsy said. "And I like it. I'd like you to make love to me."

Brad hugged her and kissed her deeply. "Oh, baby. Oh, baby."

ON DISPLAY

"You know I've studied this stuff for years," Mike told Tad and his wife, Joyce. "Hypnosis can be lots of fun. How about I hypnotize you two?"

"And do what?"

"I've got a new game. As you know, I like to watch sex. You two have let me watch you make love on occasion, from the next room. Now, what I'd like to do is hypnotize you and watch and instruct you exactly what to do. What do you say?"

"Would we remember it?" Joyce asked. A confirmed exhibitionist, she loved the idea of someone watching her make love with Tad.

"If you want to, I can arrange it."

"What if we don't want to do what you tell us to?" Tad asked, not unkindly. Mike was an old friend and both Tad and Joyce trusted him implicitly.

"It's said that no one will do anything under hypnosis that they wouldn't do otherwise, but I'll reinforce that once you're under."

"So why the hypnosis? Why not just watch us and direct?" Tad asked.

"It seems more exciting this way. I can create whatever I want. It just appeals to me."

Joyce looked at Tad and nodded. "I trust you and it sounds like fun. In fact, why don't we set up the video camera and tape the whole thing?"

"Great idea," Mike said.

They set up the video equipment and Mike took five minutes to relax slowly and hypnotize the couple. "Now," he said, switching on the camera, "you'll do everything I tell you. And you'll enjoy it and remember everything. If I ask you to do anything you don't want to do, you won't come out of your trance; you'll just stop, sit up, and say, 'I don't want to do that.' Do you both understand?"

Joyce and Tad, their voices mechanical, said in unison, "I understand."

"Good," Mike said, "let's begin."

*   *   *

This last story is about a performance in a sex club. When the story stops, you can continue with what is happening either in the audience or on the stage.

THE CLUB

"How did you find out about this place?" Marylou asked her husband, Warren.

"Believe it or not, my boss told me."

"Old man Hooper?"

"The same. How he found it, I'll never know, nor will I know why he confided in me. A sex club, of all things. I guess you never really know anyone, do you?"

The couple were sitting at a tiny table toward the side of the wide stage of The Fantasy Club. The lights had dimmed a moment before and music was playing. The show was about to begin. Neither had any idea what to expect.

"And now, ladies and gentlemen," a disembodied voice announced, "Marla and Corinne." The curtains parted, revealing two women of directly opposite coloring. One was blond and had large light-colored eyes. She wore a slinky red dress, slit to the waist on one side. The other was a brunette with dark eyes and bright red lips. Her dress was identical to her partner's but was deep blue. Each girl wore silver stiletto heels and elbow-length silver gloves. The women began to dance to the music, beginning what was obviously to become a strip show.

"Look toward the back of the stage," Marylou whispered.

Warren looked in the direction that Marylou had indicated and saw two tables covered with sex toys. The first held dildos of every shape and color and machines, only some of which he understood. The second contained bondage toys, manacles, restraints, and what looked like a soft velvet whip. "Oh my God," he whispered, squirming in his seat.

Marylou touched the bulge in her husband's trousers. "Really erotic, isn't it?"

Warren thrust Marylou's hand away. "Don't. Someone might see."

"Silly. First of all, everyone's watching the show. Second, look around you. Where do you think everyone's hands are while they watch?"

Warren glanced around. Marylou was right. At every table, couples were watching the stage while touching each other. "Whew," Warren said. "This is quite a place."

Marylou placed Warren's hand on her thigh and looked back at the stage. "Certainly is, my love."

6

LET'S PLAY WITH TOYS

Many people, at one time or another, receive and browse through one of those "in a plain brown envelope" catalogs that display all sorts of seemingly outlandish products. Some of the items advertised are battery-powered; others glow in the dark. They're slippery or edible, cheap or expensive. Sex toys.

But who buys this stuff? The answer is that many of us do, and we have a wonderful time doing it. We who buy sex toys are old, young, creative, and ordinary. We have great, active sex lives and play with our partner, or we are solitary users of sexual items and please only ourselves. We play frequently, or we bring out the toy bag only once or twice a year, when we're on vacation or on the rare occasion when we're feeling especially adventurous.

Are these products so exotic? Not really. Intriguing? Yes. And frequently, they lead to all sorts of activities you never thought you and your partner would be interested in trying.

Does everybody do it? Of course not. Would everybody enjoy playing with sex toys? Probably not. However, most people would have more fun in bed if they let go of all their inhibitions and just played.

As with every other aspect of sexual communication, you may feel that bringing up the subject of playing with toys is risky. Use a bookmark to lower that risk.

If you find a bookmark that your partner has placed in one of the stories about sex toys, relax. Your partner is telling you something wonderful. He or she wants to play, have fun, get silly. You may discover that there are more approaches to satisfying sex than you had imagined.

In order to venture into playing with toys, however, you don't have to get a catalog and spend money. There are many sex toys in your home, right in plain sight, if you know where to look and if you have a fertile imagination.

Let's begin with Rob and Kathy. On a rare evening without their two sons, the couple discovers a novel use for their children's toys.

ROB AND KATHY'S STORY

"I don't believe that both the boys are out of the house tonight," Rob said to his wife, Kathy. The boys, aged seven and five, were each sleeping over at a friend's house.

"I don't, either. I was sure that at the last minute, one of the kids would get sick or something. But they're really gone." Kathy flopped into an overstuffed chair, then suddenly shifted her weight. From under the cushion, she pulled a large toy truck. "I'm getting so tired of finding Billy's trucks everywhere I go in this house."

Rob stretched out on the sofa. "There are toys in this house in places I didn't even know existed."

Kathy took a deep breath and let it out slowly. "You know, I think I'm too much of a mother. Here we are with an evening to ourselves and I don't know what to do with it. What did we used to do before the boys?"

"I have some ideas," Rob said as he leered at his wife, "but that can wait until later. Wanna watch some TV or plug in a tape?"

"I have a fantastic idea," Kathy said, her face brightening. "Let's take a bath together, like we used to."

Rob rubbed the back of his neck and thought about the old-fashioned oversized claw-footed tub in the kids bathroom. "That sounds sensational. Lots of bath oil and hot water. I don't think we've done that since Petey was born."

"God, that sounds so good. Why don't you get us each a beer while I fill the tub."

Kathy hurried upstairs and started the water in the huge tub. She scooped up an armful of the boy's toys and dropped them into the plastic laundry basket she used as a bathroom toy hamper. Bless them, she thought, but will I ever be free of this clutter? She selected a spicy bath oil and poured two capfuls into the water directly under the faucet as the tub slowly filled. Then she walked down the hall and into the bedroom she and Rob shared. She glanced at their modern bathroom with the stall shower, grinned, stuck her tongue out, and made a loud raspberry.

Still smiling, Kathy stripped off her clothes, put on a fluffy red terry-cloth robe, and threw Rob's robe over her arm. As she walked back toward the bathroom, she heard Rob climbing the stairs.

"I found the frozen mugs in the back of the freezer. Only the best for our evening's entertainment." He put two beers on the edge of the sink, within arm's reach of the tub.

"Fantastic." Kathy removed a holster and two water guns from the knob on the back of the bathroom door and dropped them on top of the toy hamper. Then she hung Rob's robe on the back of the bathroom door. She checked the water, ran just a bit more cold until the temperature was just right, then turned off the tap. "Okay, cutie, our perfect bath awaits."

Rob quickly removed his clothes and slipped into the steamy water. "This is so wonderful," he said as he slid under the water. "Coming?"

Kathy removed her robe, twisted her hair into a knot, pinned it on top of her head, and stepped into the huge tub. There was plenty of room for her to settle into the hot water without crowding Rob. "I don't understand why they don't make tubs like this anymore." She fit her legs along the side of the tub between Rob's thighs and the edge of the tub and leaned back.

For a while, they talked, periodically running more hot water to keep the temperature hot enough. They giggled and shared the day's activities. Then, with a devilish grin, Rob reached over to the toy hamper, picked up one of the high-powered water pistols, still filled with water, and squirted it at Kathy's chest.

"That's cold," she said, laughing, cold water trickling down her breasts. "The kids filled it hours ago. Cut it out." When Rob continued to squirt her, Kathy reached for the other gun and squirted her husband. Laughing and filling the bathroom with water spray, they shot at each other. When his pistol ran dry, he refilled it from the tub and continued shooting.

Kathy pulled out the tub stopper, refilled her gun, and continued to shoot Rob while the tub emptied. As the water level dropped, the squirts became more sexual in nature. When Rob squirted between Kathy's legs, she said, "That's kinky. It feels tickly."

"And good?" Rob asked, squirting again.

"Yes," she said, suddenly still. "Very good."

Quickly, before the tub emptied completely, Rob refilled his gun. Rhythmically, he squirted Kathy's cunt with the stream of warm water. When both his gun and the tub were empty, he said, "Now you squirt me."

Kathy sat up and aimed a stream of water at Rob's penis and balls. She watched him shift his hips so his testicles were more accessible, so she squirted them with the warm water. "Good?" she asked.

"Very." He looked down at his rapidly hardening cock. "See what you do to me?"

Kathy took Rob's hand and guided it to her slippery pussy. "And what you do to me."

Kathy thought for a moment about one of Rob's fantasies. He had always wanted her to put her mouth on his cock, but she had always demurred. She had been sure it would taste and smell weird. But here? She looked into Rob's eyes, grasped his cock, and leaned over.

"Oh, baby," Rob said. "Oh, baby."

Kathy touched the tip of her tongue to the end of Rob's hard cock. Fresh and clean from their bath, the skin felt smooth and soft. She pursed her lips and placed a tiny kiss on the tip, then sucked the knobby head into her mouth.

"Oh God, baby. That's so good."

Kathy, spurred on by her husband's obvious pleasure, pulled her head back and again sucked Rob's cock into her mouth. Over and over, she pulled back and sucked.

After a little while, Rob wound his hands in Kathy's hair and pulled her upright. "I can't take too much more of that. You're too good at it. Now, I'd love to make love to you right here," Rob said. "Right now."

Kathy climbed on her knees and, straddling Rob's thighs, lowered her wet cunt onto Rob's hard cock. "Like that?" she said, a gleam in her eye.

"Yeah." He sighed. "Just like that." When Kathy reached between her legs and rubbed her clit, Rob said, "Yes, baby. Touch yourself. Make it good."

Kathy rubbed and moved her body so Rob's cock touched the places inside that felt so good. Suddenly, she felt the heat build in her belly. "It's going to be so good, baby," she said. As she continued to rub her own body, she reached around behind her, between Rob's legs, and squeezed his balls the way she knew he liked. "Oh, Robby, honey."

They climaxed almost simultaneously. Kathy collapsed against her husband's still-wet body. Moments later, she said, still panting, "It may be very unromantic, but now I'm freezing."

Rob disentangled himself and stood up in the tub. Knees weak, the two lovers toweled off, and, wrapped in their thick terry-cloth robes, wandered arm in arm into the bedroom. "That was wonderful, but fast," Kathy said. "But I got so hungry, I wanted you right away. Was that okay?"

"It was great," Rob said, chuckling. "Those water pistols are dynamite sex toys. Should we allow our children to play with them?"

"I doubt they use them the way we just did," Kathy said. "But remind me when the boys get tired of them, to save them for evenings like this."

"I'll remind you. Believe me, I'll remind you."

What kinds of things can you find around the house to play with? For a start, think about foreplay as a game of sensations. Try to begin as early as you can and allow the excitement to build throughout the day. Send your partner to work with a small piece of fur or emery paper in his underpants or inside one cup of her bra. Or fashion a belt out of a scarf and attach another scarf to the center front, draw it between your partner's legs, and tie it to the back of her scarf belt. Or tie a ribbon around your partner's wrist to remind him of the evening to come. Any of these will keep his or her mind on sex all day.

Then, for the evening, dress in old clothes with holes cut in strategic places, or put a thin gold chain around your waist. Put your clothes on over your naked body, or put perfume or cologne in unusual places. And be sure that your partner knows what you've done.

Try stroking your partner with a silk scarf, an emery board, the furry paw of a stuffed animal, or a pastry brush. Try the hot or cold packs you can find in the drugstore, or pour some honey or maple syrup on your partner's body and lick it off. Arrange a mirror so you can watch your lovemaking, or make a videotape or take Polaroid pictures. Don't, however, take the kind of pictures that have to be developed. You never know who might see them. I've heard horror stories about pictures illegally duplicated by employees and used clandestinely on calendars and the like.

Please be careful if, like Rob and Kathy, you make love in the bathroom. Take care with soapy, slippery floors and small scatter rugs. Ed and I have had fun finding unusual uses for some common household items like a Water Pik or a blow dryer, but, for obvious reasons, be especially careful to keep electrical toys, including vibrators, in the bedroom.

There are also toy substitutes that you shouldn't use, although we read about mishaps all the time. Don't put anything into your body that wasn't meant to be there. People have tried the most amazing dildo substitutes over the years—everything from carrots and cucumbers to broom handles and Coke bottles. *Don't.* Vaginal and anal tissues are very delicate and prone to infection. And please *don't* stuff edibles like oysters or cherries into your partner's vagina, then attempt to suck them out. It's very dangerous. You never know what substance is going to cause an allergic reaction or an infection or be difficult to remove.

Here's a story of a man who gathered things from the house to use on a fantasy sex evening with his wife. These are common items that appeal to each of the five senses and extend a lovemaking session so it can last for hours.

GIL AND LISA'S STORY

"You look exhausted, darling," Gil said to his wife late one Saturday afternoon.

"My boss was a wild man this week," Lisa said, dropping her coat on a living room chair and collapsing onto the sofa. "Everything had to be done yesterday, if not the day before. I spent the entire week trying to keep up with him. I think at best I'm now only about a day behind. And it took me most of my Saturday to get this far."

"You know you shouldn't have to work on the weekend," Gil said.

"We've been through all that. Once this project is finished, things will get easier. Mr. Prentiss promised, so I can stand it for another few weeks."

"Poor baby," Gil said. "I have a surprise for you. Listen."

Lisa listened. "Is that Melissa's voice upstairs?" Gil's younger sister was almost seventeen and occasionally baby-sat for the couple's three young school-aged sons. They went out so seldom that they had never used anyone else.

"Certainly is," Gil said. "I talked her into breaking her date and baby-sitting for the boys."

"What did you promise her?" Lisa asked. "A new car?"

"Nope. I explained that we hadn't had an evening out in . . . I think it was about three lifetimes ago. Anyway, she agreed. She's here until whatever time we get home."

"That's great," Lisa said, "but I'm almost too tired to enjoy it."

"Nonsense. I want to spend an evening with you, and you can't be that tired."

Lisa stretched and felt unusually refreshed by the idea of time alone with her husband. "You're right. I'm not too tired. It sounds wonderful."

"Good. I've made reservations at Mama Maria's for"— he glanced at his watch—"about two hours from now, and it's about a forty-five-minute drive. That okay with you?"

"Mama Maria's. I don't think we've been there since . . ."

"Would you believe that the last time I can remember driving into the country for dinner was before little Gil was born?"

"It sounds almost too good to be true." Lisa stood up. "Let me say hello to Melissa and the boys, then I'll shower."

"And slip into something sexy," Gil suggested. "Maybe we'll go dancing later." Gil had his plans made, but he would take things step by step.

Two hours later, Gil and Lisa were sitting at a small booth in Mama Maria's, sipping very dry martinis. "Drink as much as you want," Gil said. "I'm having only this one drink, so I can drive later."

"In that case, I'll have another. I haven't felt this good in a long time, and I'm getting a nice buzz."

"You look sensational," Gil said, appreciating the slinky dark green dress Lisa was wearing.

"Thanks. I bought this over a year ago, but I haven't had anywhere to wear it."

"It looks wonderful." Gil took his wife's hand and gave it a squeeze. "And you look relaxed for the first time in months."

They spent two hours over dinner, relishing antipasto, chicken sautéed with white wine and garlic, fresh pasta, spumoni, and espresso. "I think I gained four pounds," Lisa said, "and my cholesterol went up twenty points."

"To hell with anything that doesn't feel good or any negative thoughts." Gil listened to the small combo playing in the next room. "Hear that? Let's dance."

Lisa stood up. "I'd love to, kind sir."

They slow-danced and held each other until they were both feeling too sexy to continue. "Let's get out of here," Gil suggested. He paid the check and they got into their car.

"Do we have to go home?" Lisa said. "This has been so lovely, I don't want it to end just yet."

"I thought we'd go to my office."

"Your office?"

"It's on the way and it's more private than home."

Lisa giggled. "And what did you have in mind?"

Without another word, Gil started the car. He tuned the radio to an easy-listening station and drove the twenty minutes to his law firm. They entered the building and walked to the door of his office. "I had the idea for tonight early this week and I've been planning. Stay here for a minute."

Leaving Lisa at the door, Gil entered the office. A moment later, he called his wife in. "Wow," she said. The office was filled with candles, warming the office with their soft romantic light. Gil tuned a small radio he had brought from home to the same station they had been listening to in the car. "Dance with me," he said, his voice hoarse.

She walked into his arms and they danced together.

Gil ran his hands up and down his wife's back and nuzzled her neck. As they danced by his desk, he reached out and picked up a furry stuffed animal. He rubbed its soft tail up and down Lisa's back. "Ummm," she purred. "That feels sensational." He picked up an old hairbrush in the other hand and alternated the soft fur and the prickly bristles. "You're making me crazy," Lisa said.

"That's the idea," Gil answered.

When the radio station began a series of commercials, Gil said, "Why don't you sit for a while." He settled Lisa on the new leather couch he had recently added to his office furniture. "And I thought this would be good for entertaining clients," Gil said. "I like entertaining you better."

"It still smells of new leather," Lisa said. "I'm not *into* leather, but the smell is erotic." She lay back, rested her head on the upholstered arm of the couch, and put her feet up.

"I brought something else I thought you'd like," Gil said. He opened a drawer in his desk and pulled out a jar and a plastic bag. "How about some dessert?"

Lisa smiled when she saw that he held a jar of Hershey's syrup and a bag of fruit. "What a wonderful idea."

When she started to sit up, Gil said, "Just lie there and let me feed you." He dipped an orange section in the chocolate sauce and put it into Lisa's mouth. "Ummm," she purred. "That's delicious."

Gil continued with a slice of banana and a piece of angel food cake. "I'm going to be fat as a house if you keep this up," she complained, laughing.

"I love fat women." Gil dipped another orange section and held it to her lips. Before she could eat it, chocolate dripped on her chest above the low-cut neckline of her dress. When she went to wipe it off, Gil bent over and licked the drop of chocolate from her skin. He pulled the shoulder of the dress down and continued to lick her flesh.

He sat up and redipped the orange section. Again chocolate dropped on her chest. "I think you did that on purpose," Lisa said.

"And what if I did?"

Quickly, Lisa pulled down the top of her dress and removed her bra. "If you did, you need better aim." She dipped her finger into the syrup and painted the end of her breast brown. "Now lick that off," she said. And Gil did—very slowly.

"My turn," Lisa said when he sat up. Together, they unbuttoned Gil's shirt and removed both it and his undershirt. Then she painted his chest with chocolate and took long minutes licking it off.

"Take the rest of those silly clothes off," Gil said.

"I will if you will." They undressed quickly and Gil covered the cold leather with a few big bath towels he had put in his office the day before. Gil and Lisa spent a long time kissing and nuzzling and licking each other, until Lisa was too excited to wait much longer. "I want you, you know," she said.

"Me, too. But I want you a special way."

"What do you mean?"

Gil guided Lisa's body around until she was on her knees beside the couch, with her upper body on the cushions and her ass in the air. "I want you this way," Gil whispered, not knowing why he was being so brave.

"I'm not into . . ." She couldn't say it, and, as much as she loved Gil, she wasn't going along with something she didn't like.

"Don't worry. I know how you feel and I don't intend to do anything you don't want me to." Gil stroked his wife's clit with the tip of his erect penis. "I want to make love to you like this." While still stroking Lisa's clit, he used his other hand to push the end of his erection into her vagina from behind.

"Oh God, Gil. That feels wonderful." Lisa arched her back to allow deeper penetration. "Oh, Gil."

He pumped deep into her, urged on by her small moans and gasps of pleasure. He enjoyed the sound of his hips slapping against her buttocks. "Lisaaaaaa."

Gil reached around her body and pulled and pinched one nipple. "Yes, Gil, yes." As Lisa came, she felt Gil twist the fingers of his other hand in her hair and pull her tightly against his groin.

Gil tried to slow his movements so he could make it last, but it felt too good. "Not yet," he groaned, "not yet." But he couldn't stop the fire boiling inside of him. With one final powerful thrust, he climaxed.

Later, cuddled together on the couch, Gil asked, "Was that all right?"

"It was great. I have only one complaint."

"What, baby?" Gil asked, suddenly concerned.

She reached down and rubbed her reddened knees. "Next time, I need a towel under me. Rug burns are hell."

"Oh, darling, I'm sorry."

"I'm not," Lisa said, nipping Gil's shoulder. "It was worth every red inch of it, and many more."

If you want to acquire sex toys, you don't have to order merchandise from a special catalog. You can find toys of all varieties on a trip to the local hardware store, supermarket, or department store if you have an open mind and learn to look at items in a new way. You'll find everything from a new nightgown to satin sheets, from mirrors for the bedroom to chocolate syrup, from rubber gloves to velvet ribbon to use to tie up your partner.

Cheryl did a little shopping in preparation for an evening with her husband, Joel. And it led them in new and delicious directions.

This story is about consensual, mutually pleasurable bondage, an activity that doesn't turn everyone on. If you are excited by this and decide to try it, be sure you think everything through. Never get yourself or your partner into a situation that you can't easily get out of in an emergency. And be sure the kids are safely gone. This is an activity that a child might easily misinterpret.

CHERYL AND JOEL'S STORY

"I did some shopping today," Cheryl said to Joel after dinner one evening, "and you'll never guess what I bought."

"Okay, I won't guess," Joel said with a sigh as they finished loading the dishwasher, "because you'll tell me, anyway. What did you buy?"

"Some things to help me retaliate for what you did to me last Tuesday. You haven't forgotten that you owe me."

Joel was suddenly alert. Last Tuesday, he had assumed control of their sexual evening and had teased Cheryl for over an hour before they had intercourse. Cheryl had insisted that she be allowed to do the same to him, and she had obviously decided that this was the night. "I haven't forgotten. Exactly what did you buy?"

"You'll see. Go into the bedroom and wait for me. I'll be there in a few minutes."

Joel walked down the long hallway and into the bedroom. Cheryl didn't sound like herself. She was never this assertive. What have I gotten myself into? he wondered.

Cheryl entered the bedroom carrying a shopping bag. As she set the bag on the dresser, she said, "Let's see what I can find in here." She withdrew a bag with the name of the local discount store on it. "I was in the pet department and I thought of you."

"Is that a compliment? You think of me as a pet?"

Cheryl laughed. "That's not what I meant." From the bag, she pulled several woven nylon dog collars. "I found these, just for you. But first, you have to get naked."

Slowly, Joel took off his shoes and socks, pants and shirt. He stood in his shorts and T-shirt, wondering again what he was in for.

Sensing his hesitation, Cheryl reassured him. "You can call it off at any time, darling. You know that. But although what I have in mind is a bit offbeat, I think we'll both enjoy it. Trust me?"

Joel reached down and pulled his T-shirt over his head. "Always, darling." He pulled down his shorts and stood beside the bed, naked.

"Remember last month you bought that hank of rope and tied me up?" Cheryl asked rhetorically. She knew he remembered the night of crazy passion they had shared. "Well, I had an idea. Hold out your arm."

When Joel extended his arm, Cheryl buckled a black nylon dog collar around his wrist. "Now the other." She buckled a second collar on his other arm. "Just stand still," she said as she sat on the floor. Quickly, she buckled two more collars, one on each ankle. "Now lie down on the bed."

Joel realized what his wife had in mind, but he wasn't sure he would like being tied down. In an instant, however, he made his decision. He would go along for now, knowing that he could say stop at any point. He stretched out on the bed while Cheryl pulled a few more things out of the bag.

"I wonder what the checkout girl must have been thinking when I bought all this stuff." Joel heard the sound of chains clinking as Cheryl continued. "First the nylon dog collars, then four of these chain choke collars and these." She brandished a pair of tiny padlocks and two belt clips like the kind that Joel used to keep his keys attached to his belt. "As you can see," she said as she snapped the clips loudly, "these things have clips that open at each end."

Cheryl fumbled with the equipment, then sat on the edge of the bed. "Let's start with your hands." She opened one wrist collar and slipped it through the large end loop of the chain choke collar and rebuckled it. She pulled on the chain and pulled it over the top rail of the bed's headboard. She attached one end of a clip to the metal loop and the other to one of the collar's chain links. Then she settled back and examined her work.

"Very nice," she said. Joel's right hand was attached by the collars to the headboard, his wrist suspended above his head. "Very nice indeed." She quickly circled around the bed and did the same with the other hand.

"Oh yes," she said. "There is one more thing." She went back to the dresser and pulled a longer, black leather dog collar from the bag. "This is for your neck."

"You know," Joel said. "I feel like a fool, trussed up like this. What if there's an emergency?"

"The clips will unsnap in a second and I think you can reach them if you try. I'll leave the key in the padlock so there won't be any chance of misplacing it. Okay? If you're really uncomfortable . . ."

Joel could feel his body relax. "I'm fine and I should have known you'd have thought this thing through."

Cheryl bent over and kissed Joel deeply. "I love you, you know."

Joel felt odd not being able to put his arms around Cheryl's neck. "I know. And I love you, too."

Cheryl buckled the thick leather collar around Joel's

neck, making sure it wasn't too tight. "Is that comfortable?" she asked.

"As comfortable as a collar around the neck could be." He shifted position slightly. "Baby, could you loosen my right hand just a little? My fingers are beginning to tingle."

Cheryl did so, then looped the large ring of a particularly long chain collar to the collars on Joel's ankles. She took the end of each of the chains attached to her husband's ankles and pulled them up, forcing Joel to bend his knees. With the chains between his legs, Cheryl attached the ring at the end of first one and then the other through the small padlock. Then she snapped the lock to the ring on the collar around Joel's neck. "That's exactly what I had in mind."

"I feel ridiculous," Joel said, arms suspended over his head and legs bent, chains connecting his ankles to the collar around his neck. He wriggled around until he could cross his legs on the bed, his heels against his crotch. Lucky I'm so limber, he thought.

"I can imagine, but I don't care. You're mine tonight." She looked at Joel's cock, small and soft. That will soon change, she thought. "I also rented a film," she said.

She turned the TV on, pushed the X-rated film into the VCR, fast-forwarded well into the movie, and pushed PLAY. Immediately, the screen was filled with the image of a girl with red lips and long blond hair giving a blowjob to a man with a large erection. "Oh, baby," the actor on the screen said, sighing. "Yes, suck me."

Cheryl moved around to the other side of the bed and got comfortable. "Now be a good boy and watch the film," she said. "Pay close attention. I might quiz you on the details later."

Joel felt his cock react. Watching a beautiful girl suck someone's cock had always turned him on. "Watch how she does it," Cheryl said. "See how she sucks him deep into her throat. Watch his hips. Look, it's like he's fucking her mouth. Are you watching?"

"Ummm," Joel said. Joel, while aware of his odd position, was losing himself in the movie.

"Now what's happening?" Cheryl said as the scene changed. Two women were in a hot tub surrounded by swirling water. "Oh look. See the blonde? Hasn't she got nice boobies? So big. I bet you'd like to suck them. But so would that redhead."

"Oh God," Joel said. The movie was exciting enough, but listening to Cheryl giving a play-by-play was both exciting and frustrating. "You're making me crazy."

"Yeah, I sure am. You teased me for over an hour. Remember?" She reached over and squeezed Joel's balls, so available with his knees spread wide.

Joel was silent, watching the two women on the screen. His cock was hard and hot.

"Doesn't she have a beautiful pussy?" Cheryl asked. "Makes you want to lick and suck it, doesn't it? Or maybe stick your hard cock inside."

"Yes, baby," Joel said. "Let me fuck you, baby."

"In good time, dear. All in good time."

Joel began to roll his hips to ease the pressure between his legs, but it was no use. Everything he tried to do only further frustrated him.

"You know, this movie is making me hot," Cheryl said. "Maybe you'd better do something about that." She straddled Joel's mouth and lowered her hot cunt onto it. He needed no urging. He licked and sucked, enjoying the taste of her juices. Each time she felt close to orgasm, she levered her body up until she had calmed. Then she lowered her body onto his mouth again. It was heaven, but soon it was all she could take.

Rising up, Cheryl said, "I intended to make you wait longer, but I'm too impatient for you." She unlocked the padlock and released Joel's ankles. Then she straddled his waist and impaled herself on his cock. "This is so good," she purred. She moved right and left, forward and back, using Joel's erection to probe her body. Then she levered up and down, establishing her own rhythm. When she felt herself close to coming, she reached behind her and tickled Joel's balls. She came first, and Joel climaxed soon after.

Quickly, Cheryl released the clips that held her husband's wrist chains to the headboard. He wrapped his arms around her. "Oh, baby," Joel said, his breathing still rapid, "I don't think it's ever been any better."

"Me, neither," Cheryl said. She looked at the TV. "And they're still at it. I guess they have more patience than I have."

"And more stamina than I have."

7

LET'S SHOP FROM CATALOGS

The simplest and least threatening item to buy from a catalog is lingerie. And yes, sexy lingerie is a toy. I don't know how you define a sex toy, but to me, a sex toy is any object that enhances pleasure during lovemaking, and sexy lingerie does just that. It not only makes you look sexy but, when you wear something special, it sends your partner the message, "I'm interested in having a good time with you."

You don't have to look like a catalog model to enhance your sex life with lingerie and you don't have to purchase erotic underthings through a "sex" catalog. Nowadays, every department store carries a line of enticing bras, panties, slips, nighties, and so on. Even the home-shopping channels advertise sexy nightwear.

There are dozens of G-rated catalogs that contain lingerie of all types. Recently, several of the large catalog companies have even reached into the large malls with specialized stores that sell every kind of fun undies. Visit

Victoria's Secret (more mainstream) or Frederick's of Hollywood (from the tight and slinky to the very revealing) or look through a magazine for ideas.

If you're so inclined, you can also send for one of the booklets that feature more specialized erotic clothing. If you're not sure where to look, check the Appendix on page 255. You can shop for yourself, or share the catalog with your partner. You'd be amazed what wonderful sex can be triggered by just looking at one of the erotic catalogs.

Or you might want to do what Tim did and surprise your partner with some "gift wrap."

PAULA AND TIM'S STORY

Tim had spotted the catalog on his friend Jack's bed table when they had gone through the master bedroom to fix the clogged bathroom sink. "What's with the lingerie catalog?" Tim asked from under the sink.

"What catalog?" Jack said, twisting the wrench. "Shit! This faucet isn't going to budge."

"The one on your bed table. You know. The one with the gal in that bra-type thing on the cover."

"Oh, that. I buy Jeanne something every so often. I love to see her in sexy undies. You know."

"You buy that stuff?"

"I used to think that all women wore sexy undies, but Jeanne, well, she used to wear only that white orthopedic underwear. You know, the armored stuff with the three too-tight hooks in the back. White cotton underpants. Like that." Jack pulled harder on the wrench. "I think this is moving."

Tim didn't want to let the conversation return to plumbing. He had always wanted to see his wife, Paula, in lace and satin, but he didn't know how to tell her. "How did you tell Jeanne? About sexy underwear, that is."

Jack remembered that evening well. "Funny story. I got a catalog, like the one you saw, by mistake. The catalog, called 'Night Classics,' was addressed to the previous owner of my condo. I looked and drooled. Well, Jeanne caught me and asked my opinion of what I saw. 'Looks great,' I said, 'and I bet some of this stuff would look great on you.' Well, we looked at the catalog together for a few minutes. It turned out that she had secretly wanted to get something sexy but was afraid of how skinny her body would look. As if I cared. She was so cute. 'You think I'd look okay?' she said. 'All those models have such perfect bodies.' "

Tim pictured Paula. She was a few pounds overweight and would have the same worries. "What did you say?"

"I told her that it wasn't how she looked, although I thought she'd look fine, but it was what the underwear said that mattered. Like 'I love to look sexy for you.' You know, I wish they'd have some real-looking women in those catalogs, not those perfect size six nymphettes. It gives women the wrong idea. It took me a long time to convince Jeanne to model something for me. Then, wow."

Suddenly, the wrench moved and the faucet came loose, splashing water into Tim's face. It was several minutes before he had an opportunity to ask Jack whether he could borrow the catalog.

"You can have it," Jack said. "I have lots more. And I hope it brings you the same fun that Jeanne and I have had." He winked, walked into the bedroom, and handed the catalog to Tim.

Tim was hesitant to share his love of sexy lingerie with his wife, so he waited until the next day at work before he looked at the small magazine. His mouth hung open as he turned the slick pages. "Oh my Lord," he murmured. He gazed at panties of every kind, crotchless and G-string, demibras and bras with holes in the front, through which nipples poked. There were teddies of every description, garters and garter belts, sexy lace and fishnet stockings, and chemises in every color. There was even a page with leather bras, garter belts, bustiers, and one-piece leather teddies.

He spent over an hour gazing at the undies and selecting the ones he would order for Paula. He listed items, crossed some out, listed more. Then he selected the one item he had always fantasized about, filled out the order form, and wrote out a check. On the check stub, he wrote, "NOYB," the code that stood for "none of your business," the one they used for special presents. Guaranteed that his treasure would arrive in plain wrapping, he had the item sent to his office address.

Then he waited.

Three weeks later, a plainly wrapped box arrived with a cryptic return address. He took a little kidding from his friends at the office, but he told them nothing. He left work a little early and rushed home, the magic box under his arm.

It took several days for Tim to work up the nerve to discuss the order with Paula. It was late one Friday evening, after the ten o'clock news. They were lying together in bed, Tim's arm around Paula's shoulders. "Baby," he whispered, "I bought something for you a while ago. Well partly for you and partly for me." He lapsed into silence.

Something's going on, Paula thought. I can feel it in Tim's body. He's holding himself rigid, and he's breathing heavily. "I'm very curious," she said softly. "What did you buy?"

Slowly, Tim got up and pulled the box from the back of a bureau drawer. "I don't want you to get the wrong idea," he said. "I just want you to . . . I don't know."

"Is something wrong?" Paula asked.

"Not at all. I'm just very . . . you know. I read a book once where someone called this kind of thing 'gift wrap.' I guess that's what it is."

"Can I open the box?"

With a combination of excitement and reluctance, Tim held the box out to Paula. Without looking at her husband, Paula unwrapped the box and looked inside. It was black, something made of stretchy black lace with small satin flowers. "What is it?" she said. She lifted the item from the box.

"It's called a unitard or a cat suit," Tim said, his voice hoarse. "I think you'd look sensational in it."

Oh God, Paula thought. He wants to see me in this. He's seen pictures of some gorgeous woman with big boobs and a flat stomach dressed in this and he wants me to put it on. I'll look so terrible.

Tim saw the expression on Paula's face. "Please," he said. "For me. Please."

Paula loved her husband and would do almost anything for him. "I'm afraid I'll look awful," she admitted.

"You'll look sexy as hell," Tim said, then paused. In a soft voice, he added, "Please."

Paula picked up the bit of stretch lace and walked into the bathroom. She removed her nightgown and twisted and turned the black lace material until she figured out how it went on. "God, it's even got feet," she said. It wasn't until she pulled it up to her waist that she realized that it had a split crotch. It felt sexy but frightening.

"Oh Lord," she muttered. "I hope he really means this." She struggled into the shoulder straps and looked at herself in the mirror. Her nipples, belly button, and pubic hair were clearly visible through the lace. "I hope he sees me as I'd like to be, sexy and revealing." She sucked in her stomach and straightened her spine. "I don't want him to see what I see, a woman with twenty-five extra pounds, stretch marks, and droopy boobs."

"Are you almost dressed?" Tim called from the bedroom. "I can't wait to see you."

"Would you turn most of the lights off?"

Tim chuckled. "Sure. But I'm sure you'll look great."

Hesitantly, Paula reached out, flipped off the bathroom light, and opened the door. For a moment, Tim just stared while Paula considered running back into the bathroom. Finally, Tim whispered, "Oh my God. It's better than I imagined."

Paula stood still, looking at the rapt expression on Tim's face. He was staring at her body, his eyes roaming over her flesh. Paula watched his eyes for a full minute, then felt herself relax. "You like?" she said softly.

"You look better than I had even dreamed."

"But . . ."

"Don't say it. Just accept that I see a warm, sexy woman who lives in my bedroom, not some cold, two-dimensional woman who lives on the pages of a catalog. Come here."

Paula walked to the edge of the bed. "Just stand there," Tim said. He deliberately reached out with one hand and touched Paula's belly through the lace. "Oh God." He stroked her hips and stomach first with his palm, then with one finger. "So sexy."

Ever so slowly, Jim's hand inched up the front of Paula's body until he was swirling one finger around the darkened flesh that surrounded her puckered nipple.

"I can't stand up when you do that," Paula purred, feeling the wetness between her legs.

Tim's arm snaked around his wife's waist and he pulled her onto the bed. "Stretch out," he said, "so I can look at you."

Languidly, Paula stretched her lace-encased body and settled into an erotic pose. "Like this?" It was amazing that, with Tim looking at her the way he was, she felt like some temptress.

"Oh, baby." Tim leaned over and took one nipple into his mouth through the fabric of the unitard. Gently, he used his teeth to pull the tight bud from the soft white skin of his wife's breast. Silently, he used his hands and his mouth to stimulate every inch of his wife's upper body.

Paula reached out and touched Tim's cock, hard and hungry, through his shorts. "Take these off," she whispered.

Tim stood up and quickly pulled off his shorts. "I want

you so much," he said hoarsely. Then he sounded disappointed. "But I don't want you to take that thing off."

"I don't have to. Didn't you know?" Paula said. "It has no crotch." She parted her legs, reached down, and touched the hair poking through the opening of the unitard.

"Oh, doll, I can't wait," Tim said, his hunger now overwhelming. He climbed on top of his wife, wrapped his hand around his cock, and used the tip to tease her clit. "You're already so hot and so wet," he said as his flesh slid through his wife's folds.

"Yes, baby," she said, her breathing heavy, "do me good."

Tim waited no longer. He plunged his cock deep into his wife's pussy. A few long, deep strokes and he came. Moments later, he rolled off Paula and said, "I'm sorry it was so fast. I know I didn't make you come, and I know how hungry you still are." He reached down and ran his fingers through her pubic hair. "So now, I want you to show me how you can make yourself come."

Occasionally in the past, when Paula was particularly excited, she would masturbate while her husband watched. It gave her the sexual release she needed and Tim loved to watch. Those times, however, were nothing compared with the erotic electricity she was feeling now. She slid her fingers between her legs and stroked her wet lips.

"Yes, doll. Like that. Show me how you can give yourself pleasure. Show me, doll." Tim watched Paula stroke herself, rotating her middle finger over her clit. He reached out and inserted his index finger into her cunt.

"I want to feel you come, doll. Come for me." He added a second, then a third finger.

"Oh, Tim. Fill me up." Paula could feel Tim slide his fingers in and out of her hot cunt. "Now hold very still. Just feel." And she climaxed. She could feel the waves of pleasure squeezing Tim's fingers inside of her body. "Feel me come. It's so good."

Tim had never felt anything like his wife's orgasm. It was wonderful. Her muscles squeezed and pulled at his fingers. "Oh wow," they said in unison.

Later, when they had calmed, Paula asked, "Where did you get the idea for this gift?" Tim told her the story of his conversation with Jack.

"Do you have the catalog?"

"It's in my bedside drawer," Tim admitted shyly.

Paula reached over and opened the drawer. She looked at the cover picture and whistled. "Holy cow," she said. "I'd like to show this to the girls tomorrow morning. Can I borrow it?"

"I guess." Tim paused. "You know," he said, "I'll have to send Jack a thank-you note."

"Make sure I get a chance to sign the card, too," Paula said. "I'll be forever grateful."

Tim took the first step in opening a sexy dialogue with his wife. And as you saw, it wasn't easy for him to broach the subject with Paula. But his fears turned out to be groundless. Sex is fun, and anything that enhances it can add more spice to your relationship.

Sometimes, however, it can be awkward to be the recipient of such a gift. We don't know what to do or say. We have the same fears that Paula had. But once Paula got over the body-image problem that we all have when we try to imagine how we might look in something particularly revealing, she got as much joy out of her costume as Tim did. You can, too.

Tim couldn't have imagined what his simple purchase would do for the sex lives of several other members of the community. Let's rejoin Paula and see what happened the following morning.

THE TENNIS GANG'S STORY

Paula had been friends with Ann, Toni, and Cindy since they had met in an adult-education tennis clinic. For the past six months, the three women had been playing tennis at the racquet club almost every Saturday morning. All four had good marriages and attentive husbands who had even arranged to pool the kids most Saturdays so the women could get together, away from the children.

Each Saturday morning after tennis, they showered and soaked in the sauna and talked. They had been in the hot room for about five minutes and, as usual, Ann was holding forth about her part-time job and, in particular, her boss. Paula wanted to share her experience with the other women, but, so far, hadn't been able to get a word in edgewise.

"He's such a egocentric bastard," Ann was saying, "that whatever I do, if it isn't exactly what he wants—"

"You'll never guess what happened to me last night,"

Paula blurted out, knowing that Ann would take up most of the talking time if given the chance. "Tim got me some very unusual underwear. A cat suit, actually."

"A what?"

"One of those one-piece sexy lace things. And it had no crotch."

"You're kidding." The women thought about Tim, balding, potbellied, glasses. "Your Tim?"

Paula giggled. "My Tim. I never thought he'd do such a thing."

"Wow. How delicious," Toni said. "Tell us everything."

"Yes," Ann said, "details, please."

Paula told the women a highly edited version of what had happened the previous evening. "After we calmed down, we looked through the catalog and I picked out another outfit. If you're interested, I brought the booklet to show you. It's in my locker."

Later, the four women pored over the catalog, which contained not only lingerie but all kinds of toys. "You know, just looking through this thing makes me want to go home and jump Rick's bones," Cindy said.

"I know what you mean. God," Toni said, "I wish I had the nerve to order something. But I don't think I could do it. What would Skip say? He'd think that he wasn't enough for me anymore."

"I'd love to order something," Ann said. "I've been thinking about it for a long time. You know, you can't watch talk shows without being bombarded with talk about sex toys and how it's the wife's responsibility to keep the spice in marriage."

"I don't worry about whose responsibility it is," Toni

said, "I just want to see the same hungry look in Skip's eyes that I used to see before the kids were born."

"Let's do it," Cindy said, then hesitated. "But how would we get mail? I couldn't get some mystery envelope, even in a plain brown wrapper. It would make everyone curious. I can hear little Jimmy now. 'What's in the box, Mom?' I think I'd die of mortification. And what if someone else opened it?"

"And what about actually placing the order? I'd be humiliated," Ann said.

The women looked at the small magazine for another few minutes, then Paula returned it to her gym bag. With regrets and sighs, the four went their separate ways.

I understand exactly how the women felt about ordering sexy stuff.

A few weeks ago, while preparing to write this section of my book, I decided to place an order from one of the many catalogs I receive. As you already know, Ed and I have improvised and created many playthings from ordinary household objects, but as far as store-bought toys, we have only a few.

My first toy was a dildo that Ed bought one wonderful weekend we spent in New York City. Alone, he wandered into a store specializing in "adult toys," called The Pleasure Chest. He bravely bought our first toy and then we spent a wild weekend exploring ways to use it most deliciously.

The following day, Ed took me back to the store and, while I tried not to show my embarrassment, he bought a vibrator. Since then, we have ordered a few items from catalogs at one time or other: A beginner's bondage kit with fuzzy wrist and ankle wraps, Velcro closures, and long strips to tie to the bed (which, by the way, make great blindfolds), a few jars of lubricants, and another, larger dildo.

Recently, however, I decided that I needed to be able to tell my readers about other items, so Ed and I pored through my catalogs. Together, we selected several items and added up the cost: $175. Expensive, I thought, but tax-deductible as a legitimate business expense. (I can't wait for someone at the IRS to audit my tax return.)

The following afternoon, I found a phone number in the back of the catalog and thought about placing my order the quick and easy way. As I took out my credit card, I had an exaggerated mental picture of a gum-chewing twenty-year-old order clerk at the other end of the telephone, entering my information onto her computer terminal. I could hear the conversation in my mind.

"May I have your first item number?" she would say.

"Item number two-seven-oh-nine," I would answer.

"Is that the Venus Butterfly Vibrator?"

"Yes," I would say, slightly embarrassed.

"It's in stock. Next?"

"Number two-nine-five-two."

"Just a moment." I could almost hear the clicking of the computer keys in my head as my mental images continued, "I'm sorry, ma'am, that item isn't in my computer. Could you read me the item description, please?"

Swallowing hard, I pictured myself having to say, "It's the Super Screw Dong."

"Oh yeah. I know that item. It comes in pink and purple. Which color did you want?"

"I'd like the purple." Oh Lord, how could I do that? The movie continued in my brain.

"Okay, I've got that in my computer, after all. Your next number?"

"Number three-five-eight-nine."

"Oh good. You've ordered the Midnight Special Vibrator kit with the five extensions, including the nubby tickler. I have that one. It's really fun. Just last week . . ."

When my mental movie got that far, I gave up and entered my item numbers on the order form, filled out the rest of the boxes, and mailed it to the company.

I'm sure that the order takers at such places aren't like the one in my mental movie, but I will admit I was embarrassed at the thought of talking to any real live person. And I write books about all this, so I'm supposed to be suave and unflappable. I can just imagine how others might feel. Now, let's get back to our four friends, one week later.

THE TENNIS GANG'S STORY, PART TWO

"I figured it out," Toni said as soon as the door to the sauna closed behind her. "About the mail, I mean."

"Yes?" the three women said in unison.

"I went to the post office last Monday and rented a post office box. It wasn't even very expensive. And by the way, ladies," she added, "you can use it, too. The post office lady said that as long as the box number is correct, mail can be addressed to anyone."

Cindy murmured, "So anything you order will arrive at the P.O. box. I didn't think you had it in you."

"Frankly," Toni said, "neither did I. It took me four more days finally to place my order."

"So give," Cindy said. "What exactly did you order?"

Toni took a deep breath. "I, uh, ordered a vibrator."

"Have you ever used one?"

"Heavens no," she said, then grinned. "I used to be embarrassed when people in movies even talked about that stuff. But I'm learning fast. I only hope I have the courage to share this with Skip."

"And let's order other catalogs," Cindy suggested. "We can have them arrive at the P.O. box and whoever gets there can pick them up and we can trade them on Saturdays."

"Okay, but no hogging the good ones. If you get one, you've got to bring it in the following Saturday, order or no."

"It's a deal."

It took only a few weeks for the order that Toni placed to be filled. It took longer for her to work up the nerve to discuss it with her husband, Skip.

TONI'S STORY

"I love Sunday mornings," Skip said as he snuggled up against Toni's back. He reached around and caressed her breast. "It's so nice that the kids have been trained to leave us alone." Except for emergencies, the couple's two school-aged children had been asked to munch on some cold cereal and watch TV until their parents were up and about. In return for the privacy, the family would go out for brunch.

"Nice," Toni said softly.

"You're unusually quiet, darling. Is something wrong?"

Toni took a deep breath and broached a subject she had wanted to for almost a week. "Not wrong at all. It's just hard to talk about certain things." She hesitated, then continued. "Ann, Cindy, Paula, and I have been talking a lot about sex recently." Hesitantly at first, Toni told Skip about the catalogs and the post office box.

When Toni finished, Skip said, "Sounds kinky. Do you have any of those catalogs? We might look through one and buy something."

"Well, the truth is, I already ordered something."

Skip's eyes opened wide. "Wow. I never would have suspected that you'd be interested in sex toys and such."

"I watch a lot of talk shows about sex and that's what many men say. You have to realize that we women are liberated now and . . ."

"Don't get huffy," Skip said, hugging his wife. "Just tell me what you bought."

Toni sat up, reached under her side of the bed, and

pulled out a box, which she handed to Skip. "It's called the Deluxe Foreplay to Love System. The book said it's for ultimate sexual satisfaction."

"It's a vibrator," Skip said, sitting cross-legged on the bed and opening the box. He flipped the switch and a soft hum filled the room. "I've never even seen a real one before."

"I went through the kit," Toni said. "It comes with seven attachments. I don't even know what some of these do."

Skip pressed a penis-shaped tip onto the machine and again flipped the switch. He pressed the tip against his palm. "Feels strange," he said. He leaned forward and pressed the tip against Toni's shoulder. "Have you tried it yet?"

"Are you kidding? It took me two days to work up the courage to open the box. I feel like such a pervert."

"You know, I feel uncomfortable, too, but I'm also very turned on." Skip moved the tip of the vibrator across Toni's chest and pressed it against her nipple.

"Oh my God," Toni said. "That's indecent." She pulled away.

"Is it unpleasant physically, or just mentally?" Skip asked softly. "Now be honest."

Toni thought a moment, trying to get around her mental barricades. Skip turned the vibrator off and stroked her nipple with his fingers. "Mentally only, I think," Toni said. "Physically, it felt nice. Exciting."

"You're so great," Skip said. Again he flipped the switch and stroked Toni's upper body with the vibrator. When he touched her side, she jumped and laughed.

"That tickles," she yelled, then stifled her cry to avoid frightening the children.

"The kids are watching TV and couldn't care less," Skip said. "Lie down and let's find out where on your body this contraption feels good." He spent long minutes exploring Toni's body, deliberately staying away from her inner thighs and vaginal area.

"Except for where it tickles," Toni purred, eyes closed and head back, "that thing feels wonderful."

Skip leaned down and wet both of his wife's nipples with his mouth, then slid the tip of the vibrator through the wetness. He watched both tiny buds become hard and erect. He ran his tongue around her navel but found that the area was too sensitive for the vibrations.

Then he began at the backs of her knees and ran the plastic phallus up and down the insides of her thighs, brushing her pubic hair with the tip. "Oh, Toni," he said, sliding his finger between her wet lips. "You're so hot."

Skip spent a long time both watching and playing with his wife's body. Now his cock was huge. He wanted his wife with an urgency that he hadn't felt in a long time. He put the still-vibrating machine aside and positioned himself between her legs. "I want to be inside of you so badly."

"I want you, too."

He slid inside, then held very still. He picked up the toy and stroked her pubic mound with it. "Oh, baby," Toni yelled. "That's unbelievable."

Skip picked up Toni's hand and placed it on the machine. "You do it. I don't know where to touch to make it best. You use it." He could feel Toni's hesitancy as she tried to pull her hand away. "Please. I want to watch you explore. Do it for me."

Both reluctant and anxious, Toni took the vibrator. Skip continued to encourage her. "Yes, baby, touch yourself. Find out where it feels good."

Toni moved the tip around, touching places where she secretly touched herself occasionally. She slid it around her outer and inner lips, circling her clitoris.

Skip, his penis inside Toni's body, said, "You want to touch your love button. I know you do, but you're afraid. It's all right. I want to feel it with you."

"Can you feel the vibrator on your cock inside of me?" Toni asked.

"Oh yes, I can feel it. And I can feel your body react when it touches someplace wonderful. Don't do it for you," he said, "do it for me. Let me feel your enjoyment."

Toni touched the tip of the vibrating rod to her clit. "It'll make me come," she said, her head thrown back with pleasure.

It was taking a great deal of willpower to hold perfectly still while his wife gave herself pleasure, but it was also the most intense pleasure Skip had ever felt. "Let it make you come. I want to feel you. Do it for me."

She knew that she was close to climax, and while part of her mind considered what she was doing to be unnatural, a stronger part was enjoying the pleasures. She couldn't stop, even as she felt the waves of orgasm pulsing and squeezing on Skip's cock, deep inside.

Skip felt Toni's climax as he never had. The waves of muscular contractions clutched at his cock until he could hold still no longer. A few thrusts and he came, too, the vibrator still humming between them.

Still breathing hard, Skip took the machine and turned it off. "Oh, baby, that was dynamite."

"It sure was," Toni admitted. "But it felt wrong somehow."

"How can anything that gives us both so much pleasure be anything but wonderful."

"My brain understands that," Toni said, "but somewhere else a voice keeps telling me it's wrong."

"I know. Me, too, a little. But I think we should spend a good deal of time trying to silence all those old-fashioned moralistic voices." He picked up the now-silent vibrator. "And practicing with this little goody, too. By the way, do you still have the catalog?"

"Sure. Wanna shop together?"

"Oh, baby, you know I do."

Let's take a moment to discuss various types of adult toys.

Vibrators. I now have two types, an electric pistol-grip vibrator with an assortment of attachments like Toni bought and one I just received, a slim battery-powered, phallus-shaped vibrator that came with five different flesh-colored latex sleeves.

The plug-in type is stronger and vibrates more forcefully. However, you are restricted by the length of the cord if you want to roll around the bed with your partner. The battery type is more portable but not as powerful, and if you order a vibrator that needs batteries, be sure you have ones of the proper size on hand. It could be very frustrating to want to play and then find you have no power supply. As far as which kind to buy, to each his (or her) own. Maybe every home should have one of each.

Vibrators, many with extra knobs and short shafts on

the main column to stimulate the clitoris, come in the most amazing assortment of colors, from blue and yellow to purple, orange, and black. They also come in various shapes. I've seen birds, dolphins, beavers, rabbits, among others.

As far as the sleeves and attachments are concerned, I've found very little additional pleasure from them, nor has Ed. I find that simple vibrations and my imagination are sufficient to build my pleasure. I did have some fun covering a penis-shaped vibrator with a lubricated condom. It felt marvelous, and when we wanted to switch from vaginal to anal stimulation, changing the cover prevented any transmission of bacteria without having to stop and wash the toy. Please remember that with any internal toys, you must never switch from one orifice to another (from your body to your partner's or from an anal opening to a vaginal) without thoroughly cleaning the device.

As part of my recent order, I also bought two specialized vibrators: a Venus Butterfly, a strap-on, battery-operated vaginal vibrator with the control at the end of a long, slender wire and something called a clit kisser, a vibrating plastic contraption designed to simulate cunnilingus. Both create different and delicious sensations, and that's the name of the game. And there are many more "creative vibration devices." In the catalog I'm looking at right now they range in price from twelve to sixty-nine dollars. Be guided by your pocketbook and your desires.

Dildos. In general, there are two kinds, vaginal and anal, ranging in price from nine to fifty dollars. Both kinds come in colors ranging from hot pink to purple to black to bright red. I'm not sure why. They come in sizes

ranging from the slim-jim to the I'm-supposed-to-put-
that-where? size. They do feel different—the bigger, the
fuller. I have never found penis size any indication of my
pleasure, but I'm not sure whether others find bigger is
more fun. Just be sure that the one you choose is clean
and not so big as to damage sensitive tissues.

Because the anal cavity has no upper end, anal dildos
have a flange around the base so they cannot become
lost. Never put anything in the anus that can't be safely
and easily retrieved. If you have a problem, it is at best
embarrassing, at worst dangerous.

There are also double dildos that look like two dildos
joined at the flange end. These can be pleasurable for
two women or for simultaneous anal and vaginal stimulation.

Companies also sell several types of harnesses, which
allow a woman to wear a fake penis and fuck either a
man's ass or another woman.

Lubricants. Many of us are not as "juicy" as we would
like to be. For myself, since I passed menopause, I don't
get as wet as I used to. Therefore, extra gel is frequently
welcome to prevent discomfort. In addition, applying the
cold goo can be a terrifically exciting sensation. Since
anal passages aren't naturally lubricated at all, if you want
to try rear penetration, with a dildo or a vibrator, lubrication is necessary. Even with a condom on (see page 201),
inserting an erect penis can be painful without a lot of
extra slippery stuff—thus the need for lubricants.

Most important, never use Vaseline, baby oil, or any pe-
troleum-based lubricant, as these can be irritating to the
vaginal tissues and they break down latex condoms and
cause holes and tears.

The most basic, and the cheapest, lubricant is K-Y brand lubricating jelly, made by Johnson & Johnson. It's water-based, kind to vaginal and anal tissues, and inexpensive. You can also use any spermicidal gel sold for use with a diaphragm. They are all slippery and most contain nonoxynol-9 (see bottom of page).

If you want something more exotic, every catalog sells lubricants in dozens of flavors and colors and different degrees of slipperiness. I've tried several and I offer a few caveats.

All the ones I've tried that are advertised as flavored taste like Jell-O to me. If you want to encourage your partner to try oral sex, these products can be helpful. Try the chocolate-flavored ones for your chocoholic partner. However, if the smell makes you think of the wiggly, rubbery mass you used to get in the school cafeteria, as it did for me, that can ruin the mood. There are also odorless, tasteless products, if you prefer.

Many are sloppy and frequently get on the sheets. Most of the lubricants available are stainless, but unless you change the sheets after you make love, someone ends up sleeping in the wet spot. Try putting a towel over the bed before you make love, to sop up all liquids. The towel can be put in the hamper before you go to sleep.

Watch where you put the jar or tube down. If you are energetic, you can roll over on the container and get more slop on the bed. It has happened to me.

Many of the lubricants contain nonoxynol-9, a substance that some scientists believe may kill the AIDS virus. These claims are, as of this writing, not fully proven, but a little extra protection never hurts. However, remember that you should never engage in risky sex without a condom—with or without nonoxynol-9.

There are some lubricating products that claim to prolong the man's erection. What they actually do is numb the penis and muffle the stimulation through the use of benzocaine or lidocaine, local anesthetics. That can be either the good news or the bad, depending on your desires for the evening.

Whereas slowing a man's arousal may be fine for a man who sometimes comes more quickly than he'd like, it's probably no good for someone who takes a particularly long time. Although perfectly synchronizing orgasm isn't worth the effort, as far as I'm concerned, a couple usually wishes to climax within the same time period. So use those products as you desire, but just understand the pitfalls.

Condoms. Back in the bad old days, condoms were heavy rubber raincoats that almost totally eliminated any sensation for the man. Not so anymore. Condoms come in colors, textures, and even flavors, in one, three, and twelve packs, and are available not only in drugstores but in every type of store from K Mart to 7-Eleven. Many men (and women, too) can now ask for a pack of condoms without the embarrassment that still permeates our TV sitcoms.

Ladies, buying condoms is no longer the man's responsibility. Women who may get into a high-risk sex situation should always be prepared in advance. Although it may feel awkward, discuss it with your partner and set the condoms on the night table long before they are needed.

Dozens of types of condoms are also available through most sex-toy catalogs. One of the items I bought on my recent spending spree was an assortment of condoms, to learn which are worth the purchase price. Let me share my feelings, and Ed's, although I realize that yours may be different.

To begin with, let's separate natural skin from latex. Natural-skin condoms, made from animal membranes, may feel good and prevent conception, but, as of this writing, research seems to indicate that they *do not* protect users from the AIDS virus. When making love with your monogamous partner, if you want to use them for a different sensation or for contraception, fine, but those should be the only uses, unless and until they are scientifically proven to be effective against the AIDS virus. Period.

Ed and I tried textured condoms, ones with lengthwise, crosswise, and spiral ribs, pleasure dots, and ticklers on the end. I didn't notice any difference in the feel, but if you're curious, try them yourself for the fun of it. I do, however, like condoms that come with their own lubrication. Cold and slippery can be deliciously erotic.

Many couples who must use condoms for whatever reason resent them. There are several things you can do to minimize this problem. First, experiment with several different kinds and find the ones that feel the best for both partners. Talk about it. Second, and probably more important, make putting on a condom part of the erotic ritual, part of the foreplay. Sometimes the man can put one on while his hungry partner watches. At other times, let the woman put the condom on her partner, very slowly and sensually, accompanied by touching, licking, and other erotic sensations.

If you're using a condom for contraception or for

high-risk sex, it is imperative that it be used correctly. I
know that sounds self-evident, but many people don't
know how to use one for maximum safety.

If you don't remember how long ago you bought the
condom, don't use it. Condoms do get old and the latex
becomes brittle. A broken condom is useless. Some have
an expiration date on the package.

The condom must be put on before there is any genital contact. The pre-come and vaginal fluids that are produced with early arousal are just as dangerous as those
produced by orgasm. When the man puts the condom
on, be sure that he presses the air out of the first half-
inch or so to provide a receptacle for the semen during
climax.

The condom must be firmly in place so that it doesn't
slip off. Condoms do come in extraslender and extrawide
for men with penises of differing sizes.

You must hold the condom firmly during withdrawal
so no fluid leaks out. That means that the penis can't remain inside until it's completely soft and small. Leakage
defeats the entire purpose of the condom.

Finally, a condom should be used only once!

There are also condoms for amusement only. In the
catalog I'm looking at, there is one advertised that glows
in the dark and one that is edible. Both ads read, "Sold as
Novelty Only." That means that they are not to be used
for protection. Believe it.

You may want to use a lubricant with a condom to prevent discomfort and possible breakage. Ed and I have recently been experimenting with condoms and lubrication.
(Don't you just love research?) Read the lubricant's label
carefully. There are some slippery products on the mar-

ket that specifically state they are not for use with condoms.

Ben-wa Balls. Ben-wa balls are usually sold in sets of two. Supposedly, when inserted into the vagina, they move around and click together, causing sexual stimulation. I got a pair recently and inserted them. I felt nothing. I must explain, however, that for many years I used a diaphragm for contraception. There are experts who feel that the constant irritation from the diaphragm's ring can desensitize some of a woman's interior tissue, so maybe I'm not a good judge.

Ticklers. As part of my recent catalog order, I bought a set of six latex ticklers. When they arrived, they turned out to be condom-type rolled plastic sheaths with large, bizarre plastic shapes on the end. We tried one recently and I felt no difference once it was inside me. However, I found that knowing that this weirdly shaped piece of plastic was scraping my insides was distracting and I finally asked Ed to take it off. I have read that only the first inch of the area inside a woman's body is sensitive to touch, anyway (the controversial G-spot excluded). For me, none of those devices that tickle the walls of the vagina had any effect. But, of course, you can try everything and see what's pleasurable. Just experimenting can lead to wonderful, previously unknown pleasures.

Aphrodisiacs. There are many catalog advertisements for aphrodisiacs of one sort or another, magic products that will make any member of the opposite sex "fall at your feet." There are colognes enriched with pheromones that "women can't resist," perfumes with "secret Oriental musk oils," and many more. It's all hype. The only effect of most so-called aphrodisiacs is to set the mood in the mind.

And that's enough. Anything that tells your partner that you're in the mood for sex should strike a spark.

Stay away from drugs, from cocaine to Spanish Fly, that claim to have erotic powers. At best, they're useless; at worst, they're dangerous. Period.

Clothes. There are several catalogs that specialize in clothes for playing dress up. They feature rubber and leather outfits with holes cut in strategic places, maid's dresses with long mesh stockings, white nurses uniforms, and so on.

Ann, a member of the tennis foursome, found one such catalog in the post office box, and it was the start of a new period of sensuality for her and her husband, Matt.

ANN'S STORY

One afternoon, Ann stopped at the now-familiar post office box. Inside were two more catalogs. She glanced at the first, which seemed to list the standard array of sex toys. "Dream Dresser," the second one was called, and there was a picture of a voluptuous woman in a leather dress on the front. Quickly, she stuffed the two catalogs in her purse and hurried back to her car.

In the car, she turned to the first inside page of the "Dream Dresser" catalog. The dress on the cover was described as being made of four-way stretch patent leather-

look fabric with power-net inserts in "all the right places."
Then she saw the price: $295. "Holy shit," she muttered.

As she turned more pages, she saw red latex dresses,
chains and leather, and an old-fashioned corset in pink
satin. Then she saw it, the outfit she couldn't resist. It was
modeled by a woman costumed as a policewoman. The
central item looked like a bathing suit with a high neck,
no fabric over the breasts, and a tight waistline. It was
made from the same patent leather–type fabric she had
seen in the cover dress. The woman modeled it with a po-
liceman's hat, long leather gloves, and thigh-high boots.
She was even holding a pair of handcuffs, for sale at only
$9.50. The bathing suit was $145.00.

"And it even comes in a size sixteen," she muttered to
herself. "Dare I?" She had had her part-time job for over
a year and had been saving for a birthday gift for Matt.
She would do it. This would be a present for them both.

They had done some playing in bed, Matt pretending
that he was punishing her for something and swatting
her on the ass. Once she had turned the tables and repri-
manded him for some imagined infraction. As she told
him how naughty he had been, he reacted swiftly, pin-
ning her to the bed and thrusting his cock into her. That
had been a month ago and had made her think about
ways to change their sexual relationship. For a change,
she wanted to be the boss, to determine how they made
love. This was how she would begin.

Before she could change her mind, she went home,
filled out the order form, included a check, and dropped
the envelope into the mailbox on the corner. Then she
waited.

. The box arrived about two weeks later and she scurried home from the post office. In the privacy of the bathroom, she opened the cardboard and stared at the suit inside. What have you done? she asked herself.

She took a few days and assembled the rest of the outfit. She went to a nearby toy store and wandered around until she found The Complete G-Man Set. The box contained a badge, a police-type hat, handcuffs, and a toy gun. She grabbed it off the shelf and took it to the cash register. I wonder, she thought, what the saleslady would think if she knew why I am buying this.

At home, she wriggled into the suit, put on the hat, then wondered where she would pin the badge. Since there was almost no front to the suit, she finally settled on wearing the badge on a long chain around her neck. She liked the way it hung, falling between her bared breasts. She pulled the suit off, noting that the slit crotch was already damp. She put the suit and the police set in a shopping bag, added a few other things she had gathered, and hid the bag in the back of her closet.

Over the next few days, she bought a pair of thigh-high black stockings and added them to the bag, in addition to lots of heavy makeup, a pair of large silver dangle earrings, and a pair of high-heeled black patent leather pumps she hadn't worn in several years. Then she made one reservation at a nice restaurant and another at the motel next door for the evening of Matt's birthday.

The evening of Matt's thirtieth birthday, Darcy, their regular baby-sitter, arrived, secretly hired to spend the night. Earlier in the day, Ann had picked up the key to the motel room and put her secret shopping bag in the closet in the room. She had made a few changes in the furniture arrangement and put a few things out on the dresser for use later.

"This is so nice," Matt said as he and Ann arrived at the restaurant. "An evening out without the kids is such a luxury, and this place is great."

The food was sensational. They had the house special five-course dinner, with three different wines. After dinner, they sat over dessert and talked about the usual.

"How about an after-dinner drink," Ann suggested.

Matt looked at his watch and said, "I'd love a brandy, but I have to drive home."

"Don't worry about that," Ann said. "I have a few surprises left for the evening, and we're in no hurry." She signaled the waiter and they waited until he brought them each a brandy.

"Surprises like what?" Matt wanted to know, sipping the fiery liquid.

"You'll see," Ann said, winking.

"Come on. You know I hate surprises. Tell me."

"I won't tell you, but I'll show you the beginning." Ann reached into her purse and withdrew the handcuffs.

Before Matt realized what was happening, his wrists were imprisoned. There was a simple release mechanism that he could have reached had he looked at the cuffs carefully, but he didn't. He stared at his wife. "What's this all about?" he asked.

"We've been watching you for a long time," Ann said, "and we've found evidence that you've been a very bad boy."

"We?"

"Me and the law-enforcement organization I represent. Now, I'll leave you here for a short time while I pay the check. I would advise you not to do anything foolish. You'd look really silly wandering around with those cuffs on. Just wait for me here and finish your drink." Ann stood up and walked over to talk to the waiter.

As Matt sat, he shook his head. If this was some kind of a birthday joke, he wasn't amused. He wiggled his wrists and, although he assumed there was a latch, found that he couldn't free himself. He lifted his glass with two hands, sipped his drink, and stared at the shackles that held his hands together. He sighed and realized that the more he thought about it, the more he wanted to go along and see what Ann had in mind. There was something in the tone of her voice that excited him, something forceful and sexy.

"Now," Ann said as she returned and swallowed the last of her brandy, "that's taken care of. We're ready to go." She draped Matt's jacket over his hands so they could walk out of the restaurant without anyone seeing his predicament. "Come along." Once in the parking lot, Ann grabbed the chain that joined the cuffs and pulled Matt toward the motel next door.

"What's going on?" Matt asked, trying to decide how to react.

"I'll explain. Darcy is staying until noon tomorrow, so tonight is ours. And I have some very specific plans." As Matt started to ask where they were going, Ann said in a stern voice, "No questions. None. Just be quiet and come along."

They entered the side door of the motel and walked down the carpeted long hallway. Ann took the key from her purse and opened the door to their room. She flipped on the light and pushed Matt until he was sitting in the side chair in the corner of the room. Using the handcuff key that had come with the set, Ann opened one wrist of the cuff and reattached it to the arm of the chair. "Just stay right there," she said, "while I prepare."

Ann took the shopping bag and disappeared into the bathroom. Matt sat for several long minutes, then examined his handcuffs. He found the latch, unhooked it with his free hand, then reattached it. It was good to know he could free himself if he needed to, but whatever was going on, he was going to play along. It looked like it might be fun.

When Ann emerged from the bathroom, Matt just stared and felt his cock stiffen inside his pants. She was all in black, with a police hat on her head and a badge hanging right between her lovely breasts. She was heavily made up, so she didn't look like the Ann he had lived with for eleven years.

"We have reason to believe that you've been involved in some very shady dealings," Ann said. "It's up to me to get you to talk." She walked over and squeezed her husband's erection through his slacks.

"What did you want me to talk about?" Matt asked.

"I'll tell you all about that later," she snapped. "For now, just shut up." Ann unbuttoned Matt's shirt and pulled it off his free arm. Then she switched the cuff to his other hand and removed his shirt entirely. With some difficulty, she removed his shoes and socks, his pants and his shorts. "That's how I like you, naked." She reached down and again squeezed his erect cock and balls. "And hungry."

Ann went over to the ice bucket she had filled earlier and then wrapped in several towels to keep the ice cold.

When she opened the bucket, she found that there were still several cubes floating in the icy water. She picked out the largest cube and walked over to Matt. "This should cool you off." She rubbed the ice over her husband's chest, watching his nipples pucker from the cold. "That's good. You're not even flinching. Very strong. It will take strong measures to make you talk."

Ann took the ice cube and touched it to the tip of Matt's cock. "Yeow, that's cold," Matt said.

"Shut up," Ann barked. "I didn't ask for your opinion." She dropped the ice back into the bucket and went into the bathroom. Matt heard water run, then Ann reappeared with a dripping washcloth. "I wouldn't want you to be cold," she said. She stroked Matt's chest with the warm cloth, allowing water to trickle down his chest and belly. Then she bent down between his spread legs and licked up the drops as they ran down his stomach.

"That feels so good," Matt said.

"I don't care how it feels," Ann snapped. "I was just thirsty." She picked up the ice and repeated the cold, then warm rubdown. "Your cock is really hard," she said, watching Matt's hips move. "I bet you want to fuck me."

"Oh yes."

Ann leaned over and licked the length of Matt's cock. Then she sucked the end into her mouth and flicked her tongue over the tip. With loud gurgling noises, she sucked his cock deep into her mouth, then pulled her face back, keeping the suction. Over and over, she fucked his cock with her mouth. When she felt that he was almost ready to come, she pulled back.

"Well, I'm not in the mood yet," she said. Ann unlocked the cuff from the chair and pulled Matt up and toward the bed. She had checked earlier and was disappointed to find that the headboard where she had wanted to chain Matt was nailed to the wall. She found, however, that she could fasten the cuff to the bed frame, which she did. As Matt lay on the bed, his cock pointing straight up, one hand hung over the edge, firmly fastened to the bed.

"Oh please," Matt said. "I want to fuck you."

"I want you to suck my tittie first." She bent over and pushed her nipple into his mouth. "Now be a good boy and suck me good. The better you suck, the sooner we might fuck."

"Yes, ma'am," Matt said, extremely excited by this new side of his wife. He flicked his tongue over Ann's puckered nipple.

"I said *suck!*" she snapped, slapping her husband on his thigh. Matt took as much of her breast into his mouth as he could and sucked, alternately making a vacuum in his mouth, then releasing.

"Is that all right?" he said, adding whimpering sounds. "Am I doing all right?"

"Now the other," Ann said, ignoring his question. It felt so good to be able to tell Matt exactly what she wanted. As Ann alternately fed him one breast, then the other, he sucked. He used his one free hand to feel her flesh and pull her body more tightly against his.

When she stood up, Matt asked, "What do you want me to do now?"

Ann kicked off her shoes and straddled Matt's chest. Then she pulled a large dildo with a wide flange at the bottom from the drawer next to the bed, where she had put it earlier. She had bought the toy a few weeks earlier

from another catalog. "Maybe I don't need you at all."
She stood the dildo on Matt's chest, then inserted the tip
into her soaking cunt. "Hold the bottom tightly against
your body with your free hand," she said firmly.

"Yes, Officer," Matt said. He wondered where Ann had
gotten that little surprise, but he quickly ceased caring.
He wanted her to fuck him, not a piece of plastic. "But I
want you. My cock is so hard and will feel so much better
than that thing."

"That's none of your concern. If you're good and do as
you're told, I'll fuck you eventually. Right now, I'm doing
exactly what *I* want." She emphasized the word *I*.

"Yes, ma'am," Matt said, and reached up with his free
hand and grasped the flange of the dildo. He watched as
Ann lowered her body until the entire length of the plastic phallus was inside of her. She raised up, then
dropped, massaging her body with the plastic shaft. Her
hand slid between her legs and, with closed eyes, she
began to rub her clit. She was in heaven, so hot yet so in
control.

Finally, she stood up and tossed the plastic penis aside.
"Now I'll use your cock to give me pleasure," she said,
and climbed over Matt's body and mounted his cock.
"Don't you dare come until I'm ready."

Matt was enjoying Ann's performance as much as she
was. This is great, he thought. I don't have to worry
about pleasing her. She'll do whatever she wants. He relaxed, then found that he was so aroused that he had to
concentrate on not climaxing. Think about something
else, he told himself.

This is wonderful, Ann thought. I can decide how fast
or how slowly, how deep or how shallow. She rubbed her-

self and bounced a few more times. "So good," she whispered, "but now I need for you to fuck me."

She reached over and released the latch on the handcuffs. When Matt didn't move, she smiled. "You understand that I'm in charge," she said. "I want you to fuck me right now."

Matt needed no additional encouragement. He grabbed his wife and turned her over. "May I come, too?" he asked.

"Oh yes," Ann said, reveling in the sensations Matt's cock was producing. "After I do."

It took only a few strokes before Ann came, and then Matt.

"Oh God," Matt said, panting, "that was wonderful."

"Hold up your wrist and I'll remove that handcuff," Ann said, smiling, still wearing her police hat. She released the latch and Matt rubbed his wrist.

"Does your wrist hurt?" she asked, concerned.

"Not at all, darling. I'm terrific. Just terrific."

"Then it was okay?"

"It was fantastic. You've become a different woman since you and your friends have been buying from those catalogs."

"You know about that?" Ann said.

"Tim told me the story of how it all started, and I think it's great." Matt paused, then added, "Could you show me those catalogs? Maybe I could get something for your birthday. You know, like a paddle or something. I could use it on you or . . ."

Ann recognized that Matt had added a twist of his own, but she needed to tell him something. She didn't want to discourage him, so she chose her words carefully. "This was fine, but I don't know how much I'm up for in my new role as the police officer. I need to go slowly."

"Of course, I know that." Matt hesitated. "I just wanted to tell you that if you want to take the game further, it might be very exciting."

"Yes," Ann said, squeezing Matt's hand, "it might, in time."

Videos, magazines, and photos. Catalogs are filled with erotica that appeals to the sense of sight. There are dozens of companies that cater to magazines and/or videos. Read the advertisements with care. Many of the videos are similar, sucking and fucking and little else. I've seen a lot and most of the people in them don't even seem to be having any fun. There are a few companies that make videos with a story and with people who seem to be having a good time. Femme Productions, run by Candida Royale, is one I recommend. There are also several well-known porno stars who make movies with well-defined story lines. Marilyn Chambers comes to mind immediately. The first X-rated movie I really enjoyed was her film *Insatiable.*

There are videos that appeal to various tastes. Big-busted women; men with extralong penises; blacks, whites, and Orientals in varying combinations, lesbian, gay, and multiple groupings; bondage; toys; and so on. There's something for everyone interested in watching others make love.

There's also a new trend in videos: homemade erotica. Couples make a home video and send it to the company. A company puts one or several on a tape and markets it. Some of them are surprisingly good.

One way to find out what you like and don't like is to rent a movie at your local video store. Usually, there's a little room in the back with the X-rated movies inside. I found that the first time I ventured into the back room at my local video store, it made me very uncomfortable. But after a few trips, I relaxed and browsed with the other embarrassed people. So rent, don't buy, movies until you find out what you like and what turns you on.

S/M and B&D toys and such. Sadism, masochism, bondage, and discipline have their own toys and there are catalogs that contain a host of them. There's everything from the beginner's bondage kit, which I bought many years ago and still use, to leather harnesses, hoods, gags, whips, appropriate clothing, and much more. If you want to experiment, remember the warnings about consensuality, then shop with care. Many of the products are very expensive, and improvisation, as you've seen, is quite possible. But sexy clothing can turn even an ordinary person into an erotic superstar.

Phone Sex. While not actually a toy, I felt phone sex deserved mention here. There are hundreds of people who make a good living from making vocal love to strangers over the phone. I've never called one of these love lines, but friends of mine who have say it's quite a turn-on. Be careful, however. These calls are expensive and, since most charge by the minute, the cost mounts up quickly. If you want to make such a call, there are dozens of numbers in the back of most erotic magazines.

Toys for Guys. Many of the toys already discussed are fun for men as well as women. Vibrators, dildos, lotions, and movies are equally exciting for both sexes.

I remember a story my ex-husband used to tell about a

friend from his teenaged years who created a fucking machine. He made a wooden box and cut a penis-sized hole
in one end. He filled the box with cotton, creating a
channel through the middle. He filled the channel with
grape jelly, picked up a girlie magazine, and . . . you can
imagine the rest. If you want an artificial vagina that
looks exactly like the real thing and comes complete with
vibrator, several models are for sale in most toy catalogs.

Cock rings, worn at the base of the scrotum around
both penis and testes, restrict fluid flow to and from the
penis and testicles and can help to maintain an erection.
They come in rubber, leather, and chrome, each with a
different feel.

Ball-stretchers, leather straps that wrap around the top
of the testicles, are designed to keep testes in a lowered
position so a man can't climax. They come in varying
widths and take some getting used to. You can even buy
weighted bags that accomplish the same thing. They vary
from one to five pounds. Start with the lightest and gradually increase the weight if you and your partner enjoy
the sensation.

Dolls with oral, genital, and anal openings can be fun
for use alone or for role-playing games with a partner.

There is also some amazing lingerie designed for men.
The one that I've seen that tickled my fancy was a pair of
tiny briefs with a special sleeve into which the penis fits.
The pants were gray and designed to look like the head
of an elephant and the penis sleeve was the trunk.

I'm sure you remember the tennis gang we met earlier.
Cindy, the fourth member of the group, found that catalog shopping ultimately encouraged her to play with her

husband in a new way. And, in doing so, she found that she and her husband had similar and creative taste in toys and games.

CINDY'S STORY

For the first month after Toni had gotten the post office box, Cindy had opened the box and thumbed through the mail. She had glanced through the catalogs and found them very exciting but had been too embarrassed to mention them to her husband. Rick had noticed that Cindy seemed more interested in sex, but he hadn't figured out why.

Finally, one evening after a party, Rick asked, "Wherever did Ann get that incredibly sexy dress? She's really getting daring."

Cindy was feeling brave. "One of our catalogs," she said.

"What catalogs?"

Cindy told Rick the entire story. "Could you bring one home? I'd love to see what you and your friends have been up to." Over the next few weeks, just browsing through the catalogs triggered some mild experimentation, which got more creative with each new catalog Cindy brought home.

Finally, they placed their first order—for a dildo. After that, they ordered a vibrator and some love oil. Their collection of toys grew until it occupied a large cardboard

box that they kept hidden in the back of their bedroom
closet. More and more adventurous toys arrived at the
post office box for Cindy and Rick.

It had been almost seven months since that wonderful
Saturday morning in the sauna with the tennis gang.
Now, Cindy had, without Rick's knowledge, placed her
most creative order yet. Throughout dinner, she smiled
as she thought about the brown-wrapped packages that
had just arrived. After dinner, while Rick put little Jimmy
to bed, Cindy unwrapped the large box, checked the con-
tents, and washed a few dusty items. She gift-wrapped one
smaller package and put the rest back in the box.

"I brought you a present," Cindy said to Rick after little
Jimmy was asleep. "Here." She pressed the small box into
Rick's hands.

"What is it?" Rick asked, his breathing quickening.

"Open it and see. I think you'll be pleased."

Rick pulled off the wrapping, opened the box, and
withdrew a small piece of leather with straps attached.
After turning it around in his hands for a moment, he
smiled and asked, "Is this what I think it is?"

Cindy nodded. "It's a leather jockstrap. I think you'll
look wonderful in it. I want you to wear it to work tomorrow under your clothes. Then you can feel the leather
and think about me and sex. And I'll be thinking about
you, too." She smiled, then urged him teasingly to "try it
on for size."

Awkwardly, Rick put the jockstrap on, placing one thin
strap between his cheeks and arranging his penis and testicles in the leather pouch. As he fastened the side straps
and straightened up, he realized that much of his prob-

lem in putting the device on was that he was getting very excited.

"Wow," Cindy said, staring at his erection. "You seem to be enjoying that thing. You look good enough to eat. Come here."

He walked over to where Cindy was sitting and stood before her. She cupped the pouch and ran her fingers over the smooth leather. "So soft," she said, "and so hard underneath." She inhaled. "And it smells so good. It makes me want you. Fuck me, baby."

Rick fell on top of his wife and, pulling the jockstrap off, took little time to plunge his hard cock into her wet cunt.

Later, as they lay side by side on the bed, Rick said, "That thing feels kinky somehow. I don't think I could wear it to work. I'd have a hard-on all day."

"That sounds good to me. Then you'll be ready for me tomorrow night. I don't think it will show under your jeans, either. Do it, please. For me."

The next morning, little Jimmy sat watching TV and eating his cereal. Although Rick didn't say anything out loud, when Jimmy wasn't looking, he rubbed his crotch and winked. Cindy knew that he was wearing his leather underwear. Just as she had planned, he'd be hot for her all day. Well, she thought, you're in for a few surprises tonight.

That evening, Rick arrived home and Cindy could see from his expression that the underwear had worked as she had expected. "God," he said softly while he and Cindy were getting dinner, "I'm so hot, I could fuck you right here."

"Baby," she said, putting her plan into action, "could

we wait 'til morning?" She wanted him hot and hungry all night.

"How come?" Rick asked, frustrated and a little annoyed.

"Because I have plans." She winked at her husband.

He smiled. "Do you have something special in mind?"

Cindy shrugged. "Maybe. . . ."

"It's just that I'm so hot, I think I'll explode."

"Well, just hold on until morning. Okay?"

Rick hugged her briefly. "Sure, if you'd like."

"It'll be worth the wait, I promise."

After little Jimmy was in bed, they sat in the living room and watched TV. After the ten o'clock news, Rick wandered into the bedroom. "Just a second," Cindy called, then she quickly raised the thermostat. It's going to get very hot in here tonight, she thought smiling at her mental double entendre.

As they undressed, Cindy said, "Would you leave that jockstrap on, baby? I'd love to wake up with you wearing it. It's so sexy."

"I guess so," Rick said, his cock beginning to swell, "but it gives me a continual hard-on. I don't want to come in my sleep."

"I'll risk it," Cindy said, "if you will."

Rick climbed into bed wearing only the leather jock. "I love you, you know," he said, snuggling against his wife's body.

"Me, too," Cindy said. She kissed the end of his nose. "Sleep well."

Rick turned over and soon fell asleep. When she was sure he was asleep, Cindy slipped out of bed and took the rest of her newest acquisitions out of the box in the closet. In the dim light, she looked at the leather harness with the hole in the front and the slender dildo with the wide flange around the base. Tonight, she was going to do some things she knew Rick had wanted for a long time but had been unable to do more than hint about.

She fit the dildo into the harness and buckled the contraption around her waist and hips. My God, she thought as she looked down, it's as though I've got a slim cock. She wiggled her hips and watched the cock jiggle. Oh, Rick, I never realized that I'd find this so exciting. I thought I was doing it just for you, but I'm soaking wet already.

Without waking Rick, she turned on the bathroom light, which softly illuminated the bedroom. Silently, she padded around to Rick's side of the bed and placed a jar of lubricant and her other new toy on his night table.

She looked down at her sleeping husband. It was so warm in the bedroom that he had thrown off his covers. He lay close to the edge of the mattress, spread-eagle, his small, soft cock still encased in the black leather. Smiling, she reached down and gently stroked the leather pouch. Rick groaned but didn't awaken. As Cindy touched him softly, she felt his cock harden.

With as little movement as she could, she unfastened the snaps at the sides of the pouch and pulled Rick's hardening cock free. She knelt beside the bed so that Rick couldn't see her lower body when he awoke, then slid her lips over the tip of his cock. Then she sucked and drew the shaft into her mouth. "Oh, baby, don't stop," Rick moaned, suddenly fully awake.

Cindy continued alternately pulling back and sucking, simulating intercourse with her mouth. She felt her husband's hips buck. "Don't come yet," Cindy said, sitting back on her haunches, "I have a few more surprises for you."

"Oh God, baby. I don't know how many more of your wonderful surprises I can take."

Cindy reached behind her and handed Rick what looked like a plastic sleeve with a realistic hand wrapped around it. While he held it, Cindy took a fingerful of lubricant and rubbed the opening of the sleeve. "Slip this on your hard cock," she said.

Without much thought, Rick slipped the sleeve on. He felt it snugly surrounding his penis and the plastic hand wrapped around his cock, as if jerking him off. As Rick took a breath to say something, Cindy said, "Don't talk, just feel." She flipped the switch and soft vibrations surrounded Rick's cock. "And don't come," she reminded him.

"This is pure torture," Rick said, "but it's wonderful, too."

"Good, because I have one more surprise for you." Cindy stood up and watched her husband's face as he saw the harness and dildo arrangement she was wearing. "Oh, baby," he said, his voice hoarse, "I don't know. . . ."

"I do. I know you want this, but you won't let yourself admit it. That's why I've gotten you so hot." Rick was silent, his hard cock sticking straight up, surrounded by the plastic hand. "Let me fuck you this way. If at any time you don't like it, just tell me to stop and I will." She waited for Rick to ask her not to start, but he didn't.

"Now, turn over and slide down here." Cindy positioned Rick's body so he was kneeling on the floor, with his shoulders on the bed. His cock was trapped between his belly and the sheets. "Hold very still," Cindy said. "If you move, I'm afraid you'll come, and I don't want you to do that just yet." She took a fingerful of lubricant from the jar and spread it on the end of the dildo, the flange of which was held fast within the harness she wore. She took another fingerful of slippery goo and spread it around his anus.

"Now I'll go real easy, and promise you'll stop me if I hurt you." She pressed the tip of the dildo against his ass-hole and pressed her hips gently. Then she pulled back and used her finger to lubricate the ring of anal muscle, inserting her finger about an inch. She could feel the soft vibrations of the sleeve and hand, still around Rick's cock. Then she again positioned the anal dildo and pushed.

"Oh God, baby, it's too much," Rick groaned. "Wait a minute."

Cindy froze. "Do you want me to stop?"

"No, baby, don't stop." He pulled the vibrator from his cock. "I just want to feel one thing at a time."

"Oh, darling," Cindy said as she grasped Rick's hips and gently pushed the dildo in deeper. "You feel so good." Slowly, the dildo slid inside. When the plastic penis was completely buried in her husband's ass, Cindy stopped to let him get used to the feeling. "Tell me," she whispered.

"So kinky, but good," he said. "I feel so filled. It's so perverted but so exciting."

"It's not perverted if it gives us both pleasure," Cindy whispered. She pulled back and slid in again. "It's like fucking you," she said, her breathing ragged. "It's so erotic." She reached down and fingered her clit around the straps of her harness. "I'm so hot that I'm touching myself. I'm going to make myself come, so don't hold back now," she said.

Rick could feel the dildo in his ass move as Cindy's fingers worked in her cunt. He felt the dildo gradually withdrawn, then Cindy slowly filled him again. "Tell me," he said, holding absolutely still.

"It feels so sexy and I'm so excited. I'm rubbing my clit while I fuck you."

"Are you going to come?" Rick said, his breathing hard and fast. "Tell me when."

Cindy rubbed her clit as the dildo pressed against her pubic bone. "Baby, I'm going to come."

Rick moved his body so his cock rubbed against the sheet.

"Oh, Rick. When you move, it bounces the end of the dildo against me." He wiggled his hips and felt her body stiffen. "Yessss," Cindy cried as she came. "Oh yes."

Rick rubbed his cock against the bed and arched his back. In only a moment, he felt the semen spurt between his belly and the bed. "Oh God!" He panted. "Oh God!"

Cindy pulled the dildo from Rick's body and quickly removed the harness. Then she collapsed on the bed beside her husband. "It's never been any better," she said when her body had calmed. "That was wonderful."

"That really isn't too kinky?" Rick asked, still unsure.

"It really isn't. It gave us both pleasure. What could be wrong with that?"

"My mind agrees with you, but somewhere a little voice keeps telling me I'm sick, weird."

"We'll just have to shut that voice up. It says dumb things."

"It sure does."

And there's so much more. I've tried to touch on most of the products currently on the market, but I'm sure I've missed some. So pore over whichever catalogs you can find, buy something that appeals to you, and play with your partner to your heart's content. Have fun!

8

GAMES FOR THE MORE ADVENTUROUS

The first of the following stories combines a time-limit game with toys and an exotic and unusual setting. Notice that, as with most of the stories I write, neither Guy nor Vicky are ever described. Try to see yourself in their place and experience the evening they spend together.

Although you probably don't have a motel quite like the Pleasure Palace in your town, you can use some of the ideas to create your own night of pleasure.

LET'S PLAY A ROAD GAME

"Oh Lord," Vicky said. "I expected exotic, but this place is beyond my gaudiest dreams."

Guy, Vicky's husband, just shook his head, looking around the room at the Pleasure Palace Motel. The large central room was done in black, red, and white, with gold-flocked red wallpaper and tassels everywhere. The main room was dominated by the red-covered heart-shaped bed with brass head- and footboards and a combination TV, stereo, tape, and CD player. "JJ told me we would be in for an experience when he suggested a night at this place, but . . ."

"You know," Vicky said. "It may be tacky, but it does inspire one, doesn't it?"

Guy looked at his wife as she theatrically put her suitcase on the chair, opened it, and removed their paisley quilted toy bag. "You may be right." He looked around and ticked off the room's assets. "Let's see. In this alcove, we have our own private heart-shaped hot tub and over there is the fireplace and a furry white rug. And, of course, the bed with"—he flipped back the gaudy red-fringed bedspread and felt the bedclothes—"satin sheets. Black, no less."

"Gives one ideas, doesn't it?" She walked into the dressing alcove. "And in this alcove, there's a tray with chilled champagne, fresh strawberries, and two fluffy white robes for après hot tub."

"I know it's tacky," Guy said, "but for what we paid, we

should just roll with it and take advantage of as much as we can."

Vicky walked over to the wide sliding glass doors and slid one open. "This balcony is sensational. You can see the lights of the city, and the soft breeze is yummy. You think they have giant fans to create the atmosphere?"

Guy walked onto the balcony and stood behind his wife, putting his hands on her shoulders. "And it's completely private." He sat on one of the lounge chairs and pulled Vicky down until she was sitting between his legs, her back against his chest. "This gives me some wonderful ideas," he whispered. He slid his hands up under Vicky's sweater and flicked his thumbs over her nipples. "I've always wanted to make love outdoors."

Giggling, Vicky pushed her husband aside and stood up. "Not so fast, buster. We paid through the nose for this room and we're going to do it up right."

"Ahhh." He sighed. "The power of anticipation. Okay. Whatever you want. I'm a patient man. What's first?"

"I want to soak in the hot tub. Let's make a deal." She looked at her watch. "It's almost eight o'clock. How about we agree not to fuck until at least ten."

"Nine-thirty," Guy said.

"Nine-forty-five."

"Done. No intercourse until nine-forty-five." Guy stood up. "Hot tub, here we come."

The couple undressed quickly and climbed into the bubbling warm water. "This is luxury," Vicky said, stretching out and spreading her arms on the redwood ledge around the tub.

"It's wonderful," Guy said with a sigh. He reached across the tub with his foot and stroked the inside of

Vicky's thigh with his toes. Playfully, she batted his foot away. "Remember our bargain," she said. "It can't be much after eight-fifteen. Much too early."

"You weren't listening, darling," Guy said. "I said no intercourse until nine-forty-five. I said nothing about teasing and playing." Guy climbed out of the tub and wrapped the motel robe around him. Soon after he disappeared into the dressing alcove, Vicky heard the pop of the champagne cork. "Great idea," she said. "Bring the strawberries, too."

Guy returned with a tray containing the champagne, strawberries, and, suspended from one arm, their toy bag. He set the tray on the ledge beside the tub and put the bag on the floor within easy reach. Then he removed his robe and climbed back into the tub. "Your bubbly, my dear." Guy handed his wife a glass filled with champagne, with a bright red strawberry at the bottom. "Great combination, bubbly and berries."

Vicky plucked the red berry from the glass and popped it in her mouth. Then she finished the drink in one gulp. She held the glass out for a refill. "Not too much alcohol in the hot tub," Guy cautioned. He popped another strawberry into his wife's mouth. "More champagne when we get out."

"Ummm," Vicky purred. "I feel sensational and mellow."

"And you're about to feel much better," Guy said. "Stand up."

"Since when did you become boss?"

"Since I have some delicious ideas about how to spend the evening. Stand up."

As Vicky stood up, water cascaded from her body. She

stood, head back and eyes closed. Guy reached into the toy bag and pulled out a slender plastic dildo and a pair of stretchy spandex panties they had cut down from a pair of old bicycle pants. He handed Vicky the dildo. "I want you to put this in, then put on the panties to hold it in place."

Vicky's eyes opened and she saw what he had in mind. She took a breath to protest, but Guy interrupted. "We agreed to make the most of this evening, and relaxing in a tub wasn't exactly what I had in mind. Come on. Play with me."

Vicky hesitated only a moment, then took the dildo from her husband. It slipped easily into her wet body, but it took several minutes of struggle to get the latex panties up over her wet skin. When she was finally arranged, dildo deep inside of her, she sat back down in the swirling water. "Good?" Guy asked.

"Sexy as hell. This thing is trying to make me hungry and the warm water is trying to relax me. It's a dynamite combination."

"Try to move so one of the underwater jets sprays between your legs," Guy suggested.

Vicky wiggled and when her body was arranged, she said, "Oh God, this is fantastic. It's kind of like a vibrator moving inside me."

Guy reached over and interrupted the jet with his hand, then let it spray again. He moved his hand in and out of the jet, causing a pulsing deep inside of Vicky's body. "Not too much," she said. "It's much too soon."

"You're right," Guy said. "Ready to get out?"

Vicky stood up, climbed out of the tub, and put the fluffy robe on over her latex panties. Guy climbed out behind her, slipped on his robe, and began to rub his wife's body dry through the robe. He dried her arms and back, then gently rubbed her ribs and breasts. He pressed the robe against her hips, squeezing most of the water from under the spandex. "How about a fire?"

"But it's seventy degrees out."

"Who cares. The air conditioner is on." He walked to the fireplace and turned on the gas jet. A pilot light ignited the gas. "Not real wood," he said, "but not a bad-looking fire." He patted the furry rug beside him and Vicky stretched out on her back. Guy bent over and kissed her full lips. "You taste of chlorine," he said.

"Should I shower it off?"

"Not on your life. You always taste delicious." He licked her lips and, when they parted, he ran his tongue around the inside of her lips and her teeth. "Sensational." He placed a series of tiny kisses across her jawline and nipped at her earlobe. He swirled his tongue around the hollow behind her ear, then down the side of her neck and across her shoulder muscle.

Vicky felt her robe part and felt Guy kissing and nibbling his way across her collarbone, then down toward her breast. She felt her nipple harden.

Guy sucked the hardened tip into his mouth and rhythmically drew and released like a suckling baby. He then licked and kissed a line across her chest and repeated his suckling on the other nipple. "As I said, you taste delicious." He looked at the ornate brass clock on the mantel. "But it's only eight-forty-five. Not time for anything too serious yet. Let's have some more champagne."

Half an hour later, with a definite buzz from the erotic

scene and the champagne, the couple lay in front of the fire. "You know, you've had that dildo inside of you for quite a while," Guy said. He reached down and tapped the end of the solid plastic through the now-dry latex.

"You know, I'd gotten so used to it, I'd almost forgotten about it." Guy tapped again and Vicky laughed. "Cut that out. It feels weird."

"I think it's time for something more," Guy said, reaching for the toy bag. He withdrew a tube of lubricant and a strangely shaped dildo with two shafts and a wide flange on the end. "See what I've got? It's a new one, just for you." Slowly, he squeezed a dollop of slippery gel onto the tip of the more slender shaft and rubbed it up and down.

Vicky was unable to speak. It was as if someone had charged her body with electricity. Her eyes wide, she watched Guy's movements.

"I can see you're excited," Guy said, "because you know where this is going. Lift your hips."

Vicky was unable and, she realized, unwilling to resist. She lifted her hips and felt Guy pull her latex panties down past her thighs. "Now bend your knees," Guy said, and Vicky did, exposing her white bottom.

Guy took a bit of lubricant on his finger and touched it to Vicky's anus. "That's cold," she said. Guy ignored her and rubbed the gel around her opening. He slid his finger about a half an inch inside to spread the gel. "I know how much you'll like this," he said. "It's just the right size." Although they had never had anal intercourse, Guy knew that his wife loved it when he slid his finger inside her ass. This would be the first time they had tried an anal dildo.

"Now, I don't think this will hurt, but if it does, be sure to tell me." He pulled the original dildo from Vicky's vagina and rubbed the tip of the new one around her back opening and pushed. Both shafts slid in easily, one into her vagina and one into her ass. He pushed until both columns were buried deep in her body, then pulled out slightly.

"Oh God." Vicky panted. "That's unbelievable."

As he wiggled the two-pronged dildo around, he said sternly, "Don't come. It's only nine-fifteen, so we've got half an hour to play."

"And if I do?" Vicky said, unable to keep her body still.

"Just don't." He slid both shafts firmly into Vicky's body, then pulled her latex panties back up. "That ought to hold everything in place." Guy stood up and slid a tape into the tape player. When the voice of Frank Sinatra filled the room, he offered his hand to Vicky. "Let's dance."

"With all this stuff inside of me?"

"Exactly. Come on."

Vicky smiled and carefully stood up. She dropped her robe and removed Guy's. She walked to her pocketbook and pulled out a small bag. "You're not the only one who did some shopping. Where's that jelly?"

"What have you got there?" Guy said, handing her the lubricant.

"Something I've always wanted to try on you." She opened the package and held up a string of beads. Each marble-sized bead was separated from the next by about an inch of slender nylon string and there was a large ring at the end. She pulled on the string and tested it to make sure it wouldn't break.

"I bought some anal beads for you," she said. She put the string and the three beads into her mouth and, with exaggerated sucking movements, moved them around. Then she inserted the tip of her tongue into the large ring on the end of the string and stuck it out of her mouth. She grasped the ring and slowly pulled the string with the beads at intervals through her pursed lips. As each bead emerged, there was a sucking-popping sound. "You know where these go, don't you?"

"Oh, baby."

She wet the beads with the lubricant and said, "Bend over and grab your knees." She inserted first one bead, then the second, then the third into Guy's ass. Then she pushed them deep inside, the large ring remaining outside. "Now, let's dance."

With his first movement, Guy's ass sent an unbelievable sensation straight to his cock. Gingerly, he moved, each change in position causing his cock to harden. Vicky held her arms open. "Now we both know how it feels."

Guy and Vicky danced, surrounded by erotic sensations. "This is making me crazy," Guy said.

"Don't come," Vicky said, imitating Guy's voice of earlier. "It's only nine-thirty, so we've still got fifteen minutes."

"I don't know whether I can wait. Not with you rubbing your body against me like that."

"Let's go out on the balcony," Vicky suggested. "Maybe that will cool us off." As they walked through the sliding door, Vicky felt her nipples react to the cooler air.

Guy looked at Vicky's body. "Cool us off? Maybe we should just get ready to make love."

"We've been making love for the last few hours," Vicky said.

"I stand corrected. You're right. But now I think it's time for me to pull off these panties." He knelt at his wife's feet and pulled down the undies, using one hand to keep the dildo in place. When her legs were free, he said, "There's one more thing I want to do." He reached up and, after giving it a few thrusts, pulled the dildo out of her body. He settled her on the lounge chair, then lubricated and inserted a new device into her ass. Then he twisted the base.

"Oh my God," Vicky said as the motor hummed. She spread her legs. "That's so erotic. It makes me want you. Please. Fuck me, baby."

"But I'm not sure what time it is."

"Forget the time and stick that big cock of yours into me."

Guy obliged by kneeling on the end of the lounge chair, grasping his cock, and pressing it into his wife's soaked cunt. "Like this?" he asked.

"Oh yes. Just like that. Now, fuck me good."

Guy levered his body up and down, thrusting into his wife's body. "Oh, baby," Vicky said, "I'm going to come." She reached down between their bodies and rubbed her clit. "Don't stop," she said as she felt her orgasm flow from her belly. The sensations from the anal vibrator were now too intense, so she raised her hips, pulled it out, and dropped it onto the balcony. Then she awkwardly reached around her husband's body and fumbled for the ring at the end of the string of beads.

"Oh yes, baby," Guy said, grabbing the ring and putting it in her hand. "Do it. I'm going to shoot."

When she felt the familiar spasms in Guy's body, she grasped the ring and pulled the beads from his body, one by one. "Yes," he screamed. "Yes, yes, yes." The beads joined the vibrator on the floor of the balcony as Guy spurted.

Guy collapsed on top of Vicky, his breathing harsh and rapid, his pulse pounding in his ears. It was several minutes before they both calmed down. Smiling at his wife, Guy stood up and gathered the toys that were scattered about. Arm in arm, they walked into the bedroom, dropped on the bed, and were asleep almost instantly.

The following morning, Vicky nudged Guy awake. "Hey, baby," she said, "did you notice what time checkout is?"

"I think it's noon."

"Good. It's only seven-thirty. Maybe we can grab a bite of breakfast and be back here by nine. Then we'll be able to make love all morning."

"Sounds great," Guy said. "I find myself hungry for so many things."

Sex by remote control has always been a particularly delicious fantasy of mine. This story concerns toys that, to the best of my knowledge, don't exist. If they did, however, I'd be the first on line to buy them. If anyone knows of any toys like these that are currently on the market, please write to me at the address on page 259.

LET'S PLAY BY REMOTE CONTROL

Herb spent most of his time puttering around in his workshop. As long as he had been married to Diana and, according to Herb's mother, from the time he was old enough to use a screwdriver, Herb had been an amateur inventor. Although he had worked for the last twelve years with the local phone company, he spent considerable time in his workshop.

He had once created a new can opener that everyone conceded worked better than any other on the market. Unfortunately, when he delved into the economics of the project, he discovered that it would cost $450 to produce and had a life expectancy of only about one thousand cans, so it never got off the ground.

He had invented an electronic doghouse door, controlled by a pendant attached to the dog's collar. Sadly, it wasn't totally dog-proof, and one afternoon during final testing, his neighbor's poodle got quite a shock. In addition, every time the poodle entered or left his doghouse, three garage doors in the neighborhood opened and closed several times.

Once, however, Herb did obtain and subsequently sell a patent for an improvement for electronically operated car windows. He had used the money to buy more electronic equipment.

For the last several years, he had been delving into remote control. Using the works from radio-controlled car models, television sets, and garage-door openers, he created devices that would turn on his house lights and the TV set from his car as he arrived home from work. He was now working to adapt his electric toothbrush to remote control, although he hadn't figured out exactly why yet.

Diana, his wife of six years, indulged his hobby. It kept him occupied while she corrected papers for her seventh-grade math class. Occasionally, it even earned some extra money. Although she wasn't very knowledgeable about electronics, from time to time Herb asked her help on a project. Recently, however, he had been working in the garage on a "secret project" that he had told her nothing about except that it would be ready for a "test drive" that weekend.

Saturday afternoon, Herb called Diana into the bedroom. "I've got a new product I want to test out on you," Herb said. "It's a little unusual, but I think it's a real money-maker. And it will be a lot of fun to try."

"What is it?" Diana asked.

"It's a little hard to explain," Herb said. "I've invented some sex clothes."

Diana started to laugh. "You always did have an evil little mind, darling, but sex clothes? You mean lingerie?"

"Not exactly, but you'll see. And what could be more natural than combining my two favorite things: sex with you and electronics?" He held up a bra and a pair of underpants. The bra was black and a bit heavier than the ones that Diana usually wore. When Herb put it into Diana's hands, it felt a bit bulky and stiff and there were a number of thick places where she could feel something small and metallic sewn into the fabric. "What's in here?" she asked.

"Tiny batteries, like those they use in hearing aids. And some receivers and tiny control units." He handed her the pants, made of the same material, with the same kind of thick spots.

"You don't intend for me to wear this, do you?"

Herb just grinned at his wife, baring his white teeth. "Of course I do, my dear."

Diana was intrigued. They had an active and creative sex life, replete with a toy box filled with goodies. But this? "Are you sure I won't electrocute myself with any of this?"

"I'm sure. I've tested both pieces thoroughly, and everything here is entirely safe. The only thing I haven't been able to test is the effect. And since I want to give it a good test, I'd like it if you would wear it to the movie tonight." They had plans to go to a new movie that Diana had wanted to see since she had first heard about it.

Diana was always ready to experiment, so she put on the undies. They fit well and didn't feel too uncomfortable, but the bra and panties were a little lumpy, so she covered them with a loose-fitting black sweater and a long, full peasant skirt.

"Ready, darling?" Herb called from the front door. "If we're going to eat at the Hunan restaurant in the mall, we'll have to hurry."

"Coming." Diana hurried downstairs and slipped her coat on.

"How do they feel?" Herb asked.

"I'd almost forgotten. They don't feel particularly different. Just a little bulky. A lot of fabric in the crotch especially."

"I'll have to see whether I can fix that," Herb said.

The couple climbed into the car and Herb pressed a button on the dash. The lights in the house went out, the burglar alarm set itself, and the answering machine snapped on. "Let's go."

Throughout dinner, Diana did most of the talking, since Herb couldn't keep his mind off the undies that he knew Diana was wearing. Diana, on the other hand, seemed to have no such problem. It seemed to Herb that she had forgotten about his experiment. Just as well, he thought. This way, I'll have an unbiased opinion.

They entered the movie theater only moments before the start of the picture and found seats way toward the front, where Diana liked to sit. "I love to have the picture surround me," she said. "Many people find this hard on the neck, but I love it."

Herb looked around. There were no people for several rows behind them.

The movie was set during World War II, with lots of gunfire and bombs, perfect for what Herb had in mind. He turned and saw that Diana was thoroughly immersed, lost in the desert of 1942 North Africa. He slipped his hand into his pocket and found the tiny remote device, a box the size of a pack of cigarettes with several knobs and switches on it. He turned a control knob a quarter turn.

"Oh my God," Diana said in a stage whisper. "What's that?"

"What's what?" Herb asked, turning the knob back off.

"I felt . . . I don't know. A buzzing. A sound or a feeling, I'm not sure."

"I didn't feel anything," Herb said. He was happy to note that he hadn't heard anything, either, over the sound track of the movie.

Diana shook her head and turned back to the film. When Herb felt his wife's body relax, he again turned the knob. "There it is again," Diana said. "In my nipples. Like a hum."

"You feel something?" He turned the control off.

Diana turned and looked at him. "It's you. You're doing something with that funny underwear."

"Okay, you're right. Does it hurt?"

"No, not really. It just feels weird. And it's very distracting."

"I want you to ignore everything and concentrate on the movie. Just pay no attention."

Herb could see her annoyance in her body language as she turned back to the movie. He smiled to himself. This would indeed be a fine test of his devices. He turned the knob, activating the tiny vibrating motors in the cups of the sex bra.

"Damn you," Diana said, feeling her nipples tighten. "I want to watch this movie. Whatever you're doing, you can play later, at home. I'm not in the mood." She turned in the seat until her back was to him. "You can do whatever you please, I'm going to take no part in anything." She curled her knees up and fastened her eyes on the screen.

Herb held the knob in his hand. He turned it up high, then lowered it very slowly. He changed the speed of the vibrating motor several times and watched his wife try to ignore the buzzing against her breasts. He flipped a switch and turned the knob. The buzz was concentrated in her right breast. He flipped it again and it switched to her left. She moved in her seat, trying to get comfortable, trying to ignore the heat flowing through her body.

"Stop that," she whispered. "Please, cut it out. I can't concentrate while you're doing that."

"Does it make you hot?" Herb asked.

She let out a long sigh. "You know it does." She licked her lips.

Herb flipped a switch and the buzzing stopped. After a moment, he said, "You miss it, don't you? It kind of leaves you hanging, all excited and nowhere to go."

Diana smiled and nodded. "It does, but I'll have to settle for the movie." She pointed at her bra. "Then, when we get home, you can play with this thing some more. It might be fun."

"Okay. No more bra buzzing. I promise. Not till we get home, or you ask for it."

Diana leaned over and kissed Herb lightly on the cheek. "I love you," she whispered into his ear, "and you know I'm always ready for kinky sex. Just let me watch the rest of the movie and we can rush home."

Herb put the remote device in his jacket pocket and watched the movie. The action was building toward the climax, a bombing and gunfight in an old château in France. When he had made the promise to his wife, he had fully intended to leave her alone until they got home, but now he couldn't resist the urge to play once more. He flipped a switch on the back of the control and turned the knob a tiny bit.

Diana turned in her seat. Suddenly, all she could think about was how hot her pussy was. She stretched her legs and spread her thighs. Then the buzzing started. "Oh God, I should have known. You put something in the crotch of those panties."

With one hand holding the remote control, Herb put his other arm around Diana's shoulders and touched her breast. "I can imagine what you must be feeling, hot, hungry, wide open, and wet."

Diana was beyond thinking. All her senses were concentrated on the heat and the vibrations between her legs.

Herb pinched her nipple through the sex bra and whispered, "You can't ignore it, can you? You want to watch the movie, see the hero shoot all the bad guys, but you can't concentrate. I control your panties and I control your reactions." He turned a knob and a vibrating button that lay in the panties exactly over Diana's clit started to hum.

Herb is right, Diana thought. I can't think about anything but the erotic feelings in my tits and pussy. She slid down and stretched her legs under the seat in front of her and pulled up her skirt.

"Don't forget, we're in a crowded theater," Herb said. He looked around. There were a few people in the nearby seats, but none closer than four seats away.

Diana sat up and straightened her clothes. I have to retain some semblance of decorum, she thought, however hard it may be.

Herb increased the buzzing, two tiny vibrators alternated pulsing, one near her cunt lips and one against her clit. "I'm going to make you come, baby," Herb whispered. "But you know how you scream when you climax. You'd better think about controlling that here."

Diana was beyond thought. Her hips were twisting, unable to resist the vibrations. She felt the familiar pressure building in her lower belly, spreading to her thighs and finally to her cunt. Herb flipped the switch and the nipple vibrators hummed. "Oh God," Diana said. Herb watched her hips buck and her head drop back.

As she came, Diana tried to swallow her cries, sucking her fist into her mouth. She came for what seemed like minutes, with Herb controlling the vibrations in her body. Slowly, she calmed down. Herb handed her a tissue and she slipped it under the crotch of the panties to absorb her juices. As she returned from her orgasm-induced trance, she heard the music playing over the credits at the end of the movie.

"Holy cow," she said. "You've invented a gold mine. I've never felt anything like that. Men and women would pay hundreds of dollars for an orgasm machine."

"I'm not sure I've got it perfected yet. How about we go home and try it again. And," Herb said, suddenly shy, "I've also created a man's version. Maybe. . . ."

Diana picked up her pocketbook. "Let's get home, Mr. Wizard."

The last story involves foreplay in a public situation. Being watched or having others know you're making love can be an exciting turn-on for some, and a turnoff for others. If you want to play a game like this, be sure your partner concurs, then select your time and place carefully. You don't want to embarrass anyone else, and you don't want to put you and your partner into too awkward a situation. Remember, everything in moderation.

LET'S PLAY MASTER AND SLAVE

Karen and Max had been full-time roommates for just over four years. They had a marvelously creative sex life and each was always ready to try something new.

One evening, they arrived at a new Italian restaurant in the downtown area to enjoy a rare evening out. With both Karen and Max holding down full-time jobs and going to school nights, they seemed to have no time together.

They ordered and consumed a bottle of Chianti Classico while feasting on antipasto, fettucini with cream sauce, and veal piccata.

"That was some meal," Karen said, "and this was a fantastic idea. I'm more relaxed than I have been in months." The waiter arrived with a dessert menu. Karen opened the listing and peered at the array of fattening confections. "Okay. What's for dessert?"

"You," Max said.

Karen giggled. "I mean right now, silly."

"That's what I mean, too." The waiter returned. When Karen started to order, Max said to him, "We'll share a piece of apple pie with vanilla ice cream. And bring us two coffees. American coffees."

"Oh, Max. I love it when you're masterful," Karen said with a sickly sweet smile. "What's with the Neanderthal routine?"

"Well, that's what you would have ordered anyway, and I just want to set the right tone."

"Exactly what does that mean?"

"I want you to follow my instructions to the letter."

Suddenly, Karen understood. A game, and judging from the gleam in Max's eye, a game Karen wanted to play. "Like what?"

"I want you to go into the ladies' room and take off your panty hose, your panties, and your bra. Then I want you to bring them back to the table and put them right here." He patted the red-and-white-checked tablecloth right next to his water glass.

When Karen hesitated, Max added, "Right now."

Karen smiled and rose. "Yes, sir. Slip, too?"

"Slip, too."

In the ladies' room, Karen went into a stall and stepped out of her high-heeled pumps. She unzipped the back of her black dress. She pulled it and her slip off and removed her hose and underwear. She looked over her body. More flesh than she wanted, but it was well shaped. She just wished she was firmer.

She put her dress back on and adjusted the neckline as best she could to make up for her bralessness. As she slipped her hose, slip, and undies into her purse, she realized that the crotch of her pants was soaked. She really loved it when Max took control. As she walked back to the table, she felt weird. Not since she was sixteen and developed a 36C bustline had she appeared in public without a bra.

As Karen crossed the crowded dining area, she kept looking down at her jiggling breasts. Her large, erect nipples made impressive bumps in the knit fabric. When she returned to the table, Max's eyes roamed over her body. She started to sit on her side of the booth, opposite Max. "Sit next to me," he said. When Karen didn't react immediately, he said, "Now!"

Trembling with excitement, Karen moved over and sat next to Max. "Your underwear," Max said. He tapped the tablecloth. "Right here."

"Max, you can't mean that."

"Are you arguing?"

"No. I just mean that, well, everyone will see."

Max tapped the tablecloth again and Karen took her underwear out of her purse. She squeezed the fabric into as small a ball as she could and put it where Max had indicated. "That's a good girl," he said as he unfolded the ball and pulled out Karen's tiny panties. Slowly, he spread the bit of material on the table.

"Come on, Max," she said. "Behave."

He shook his head, then reached over and playfully pinched one of Karen's nipples. "Lift up and slide your dress up so that you're sitting directly on the plastic seat. And don't argue."

Karen did as she was told. "That's cold." She giggled as her bottom settled back onto the cold plastic.

Her tight skirt rode high in the front, so she carefully arranged her light blue cloth napkin and the fall of the tablecloth across her lap. She had just finished when the waiter arrived with their pie. As he reached across Karen and put the pie on the table between them, he couldn't help but see the panties spread on the tablecloth. He stared at the panties, then at Karen. Although she blushed a bright shade of red, she said nothing. Silently, with a smirk on his face, the waiter straightened up and walked away.

"You know that we'll never be able to come here again," Karen said, tasting the pie.

Max winked. "Do we really care? The pasta wasn't very hot and the veal was tough."

Karen giggled. "The pie's terrible, too."

"Now, about that cloth you have arranged over your lap," Max said. "Move it aside. I want to see your pussy."

"But Max, the waiter will be back with our coffee."

"Move that cloth. I won't say it again."

Karen stared at Max. In the beginning, this was deliciously naughty, but now he was carrying things a bit too far. "Max. I don't think so."

"Karen, you know you're a bit of an exhibitionist. Let's give the waiter a thrill." He winked again, knowing that Karen really wanted to do what he had told her to. She just needed to be convinced. "And it's not your decision, so whatever happens isn't your fault. Now, I told you to do something." He looked at her, knowing that, if he had gone too far, she would say so.

Karen thought about it. She knew that she could holler uncle if she wanted to, but somehow, deep inside, she didn't want to. She moved her napkin and the tablecloth aside and looked down. She could see tiny wisps of her curly pubic hair. And she could see her large breasts down the neckline of her dress. Holy cow, she thought. I'm almost naked.

"Slide the napkin underneath you. I wouldn't want your soft, warm flesh against that unsanitary plastic." Karen did as she was told.

"Spread your legs wide."

Karen stared at Max, then shifted her knees.

"Wider." When Karen didn't respond quickly enough, he raised one eyebrow.

Karen glanced at her watch, then looked around at the nearby tables. It was late enough that most of the tables were empty and the busboys were removing used dishware. Each of them glanced surreptitiously at her as they passed the table. The waiter had obviously told everyone what was going on.

What the hell. So what if a few people saw her body? They'd never have to come here again.

Karen made her decision. "Yes, sir," she said. She spread

her legs wide apart, resting her soaked pussy lips on the light blue napkin. As she looked up, she saw the waiter returning with their coffees. Oh God, she thought. Do I really want to do this? Hell yes. She felt great and *so* sexy.

The waiter's hands shook as he put the coffees on the table and he stared quite openly at Karen's body. It took almost a full minute for him to put two filled cups down, put cream and sugar in the center of the table, and fumble with spoons.

When he had finally gone, Max reached over and ran his index finger through Karen's pubic hair. "You're so wet," he said. "You must be very hot." He wiggled his finger through the folds of her cunt and rubbed his fingertip over her clit. "So swollen and so hot." He settled back. "It's my turn now," he said. "I want you to unzip my pants and take out my cock. It's so big and hard that I'm getting very uncomfortable."

Karen sipped her coffee and considered. This was getting a bit out of hand. "Let's finish our coffee and continue this in the car. I'm getting very uncomfortable."

"Are you deliciously uncomfortable or is it spoiling the fun?" Max asked.

Karen thought about it, then said, "It really is spoiling it." She pulled her skirt down. "Why don't you get the check and let's get out of here?" Max quickly signaled the waiter.

They quickly finished their coffee and paid the check. As the waiter took their credit card, he looked disappointedly down the neck of Karen's dress at her breasts. "Sorry," Max whispered to him. "Show's over."

Max folded Karen's undies and put them in his jacket pocket. He reached over and pinched Karen's nipples until they were clearly visible through the knit of her dress. "I want everyone left here to know how hot you are," he said.

When the waiter returned with the receipt, Karen slid out of the booth and walked proudly toward the door. Her large breasts with their erect nipples jiggled as she moved. At the front door, the maître d' stared at them both. The waiter had obviously alerted everyone left in the place, but Karen didn't really mind. She was proud of the fact that she and Max had such a great life together.

They crossed the parking lot and Max opened the car door for her. After she climbed in, Max got into the driver's seat. He started the engine and pressed the button to open the convertible top to the warm summer evening. Then he slid the seat back as far as it would go. He lifted his hips and pulled down his pants and shorts. His cock stood up straight and hard. "Right here, baby," he said, pointing to his lap.

Karen lifted her dress and impaled her hot, wet pussy onto his hard cock. "Now," he rumbled, "fuck me hard and fast."

"But someone might see us," she said.

"It's dark, and there's no one around. Just do it."

"Yes, sir." She raised up on her knees and pressed back down onto his cock. Again and again, she drove his cock inside until she knew he was close to coming. "Yes, master," she said, knowing that the words would inflame him. "I'll do whatever you want. I'll make you come." She raised up slowly while simultaneously clenching her vaginal muscles. She felt his hips buck once, then he was spurting deep inside of her. She settled into his lap and held him, his cock still inside.

"You're such a good girl," he said. "Do you want it?"

She wanted to scream yes, but instead she said the

words she knew he wanted to hear. "Only if it will make you happy."

"It would." He reached between their bodies and rubbed and stroked her until he felt her vaginal muscles respond. "I can feel how hot you are," he murmured, gently kissing her mouth and throat while rubbing her clit. "Oh, baby, come for me." His voice was soft and loving, urging her on. "Feel the pleasure centered in your pussy. Feel how wet and slippery you are, how tightly you can squeeze my cock. I'll try to keep it hard for you."

"Oh, baby, I love you."

"And I love you and I love giving you pleasure." His voice was soft and almost hypnotic. "Feel me stroking you. It must be hard not to come, but I can feel you holding back. The pleasure must be almost too much. I know you don't want it to end, but you can't stop the orgasm. Feel it pushing down your cunt."

Karen's back arched and she cried out. "Yes, now." She slammed her hips hard against him and her entire body spasmed.

"That's so good, baby." Max sighed. "I love to watch you as you come. Yes, baby." As he felt her body relax, he wrapped his arms around her and held her against him. "Darling, I love you so."

"And I love you. And I love it when you're masterful."

"It's hard to believe that we have something so terrific."

"But I do believe it." She grabbed a handful of tissues from her purse and cleaned them both as best she could. "Let's go home, darling."

Max put the car in gear and drove out of the parking lot.

CONCLUSION

Games, toys, role playing, sexual experiences with a capital *E*. All are wonderful, but are they for everyone? I think that there's something in this book for every sexually active person.

Are they for every day? I think not. I remember one of the first times that Ed and I got deeply into fantasy. We teased, played, and enjoyed each other for an hour and a half until the lovemaking session culminated with a potent orgasm for each of us. For weeks thereafter, our lovemaking was nice but ordinary. "It scares me," I remember saying to Ed while we were lying in bed. "I'm worried that if we start something like we did a few weeks ago, it will be a disappointment."

"I know," Ed said. "I'm afraid that we will never be able to duplicate what we had. On the other hand," he continued, "it's as if we discovered a new toy, and I'm worried that we'll play with it so much that we'll become bored with it."

Neither turned out to be true. Ed and I have found a balance between comfortable, predictable sex, which is warm and very rewarding, and wild, fantasy-filled sex that's like fireworks and champagne. I guess it's like food. Fancy foreign food can be wonderful and different, but it will never take the place of good old beef stew. Both are wonderful and each has its place.

Play as frequently or as seldom as you wish. Find a game you enjoy or a toy that's fun to play with and savor those lovemaking sessions. But enjoy your other encounters, the soft, gentle, predictable ones, too. Whatever you do, share your pleasures, communicate, and continue to explore each other. Investigate the myriad sexual experiences open to sexual, sensual couples.

Remember: Sex is fun. Go for it.

Dear Reader,

As always, I'd love to hear from you with suggestions for my next book. Please write to me and share your reactions to my current books, or let me know of changes and/or additions you'd like to see in the future, or just tell me your favorite fantasy. Obviously, everything you tell me will remain between us.

Thanks in advance for your help.

JOAN ELIZABETH LLOYD
c/o Warner Books, Inc.
1271 Avenue of the Americas
New York, NY 10020